Paving The Highway To

Success

From Home

Paving The Highway To

Success

From Home

A motivating guide formulating
successful remote working strategies

SORAYA REBELLO

PARTRIDGE

To order additional copies of this book, contact
Partridge India
000 800 919 0634 (Call Free)
+91 000 80091 90634 (Outside India)
orders.india@partridgepublishing.com

www.partridgepublishing.com/india

Contents

Acknowledgements

This book reaches out to organisations seeking to adopt a Work From Home culture and all individuals struggling to have a good work-life balance. There are many ideologies and real-life examples that can make the content of this book truly valuable, especially for women who are struggling to strike a balance between their commitment towards home and the office.

I am truly grateful to my employers and promoters whose exemplary leadership, warmth and support has driven me to become multi-talented. I owe them big in life.

This book is an outcome of the incessant support of my husband and daughter. They not only accepted all my dreams with open arms but also encouraged me to go out and achieve them. I give full credit to my daughter for conceptualising the cover page.

I can't thank my parents, sister and brother enough for having faith in all my decisions, the multiple teams that I have worked with across different cities and all those stakeholders in my professional life who are not just business partners but have also become friends.

Gratitude to all the lovely people I met on this wonderful journey called life, be it socially or professionally, I have learnt so much from them and many have inspired me to pursue my passion for writing.

I hope this book can bring inspiration and courage to all those battling the decision of Work From Home as well as professional insecurities. Putting this book together has been a daunting task, but the satisfaction that I have achieved during this period has been truly fulfilling.

As the famous idiom articulates 'Every cloud has a silver lining', COVID-19 gave me the courage to pen down this book and I am hoping it can add value to all those who read its pages.

1

Defining Success

The definition of success differs from person to person. Some people define it as power, position and bank balance, others define it in terms of popularity, fan following and so on. Success can also mean setting certain goals in life and being content on achieving them. Very few people equate success to happiness.

Success for different people can range differently on Maslow's hierarchy. A poor man who can't make ends meet feels successful when he can deliver basic needs like food, shelter and clothing to the family. Others feel successful once they meet safety and security needs, some may feel successful once they achieve social needs and most people feel successful when they meet self-esteem needs. However, there is a small percentage that feels they have achieved self-actualisation. This can be achieved even if they do not score 100/100 in self-esteem. To them, success equals happiness or a feeling of contentment in life because they have learnt to garner every moment of their life in peace, love, sharing, forgiveness and happiness. To them, it does not matter whether their business or bank balance grows, whether they will get their next promotion or increment or whether they have achievements beyond power, position and money.

This may be because self-realisation hits them early in life. Such people are not influenced or threatened by circumstances. They live life on their own terms and conditions, taking risks for the decisions they make. They are not suicidal or show-offs. They have a good balance of intellectual, emotional and spiritual quotients. However, reaching this point may take years of endurance and determination and one has to genuinely want to look at life differently as there are many challenges that come one's way. Economics teaches us the clear difference between needs and wants. Each individual must figure out as to what value of these they want to achieve and all the factors that play along the way to achieve them. There is nothing wrong or right in wanting everything in life, but there must be a point in everyone's life where they feel that they have achieved success. When this point of happiness sets in, every profession truly becomes a passion and one looks forward to waking up every morning with a sparkle in their eyes, ready to take on the universe with courage and pleasure no matter what the odds are.

In the business world, success as we all know cannot be achieved only by hard work. It requires discipline, commitment, credibility, flexibility, innovation and a right attitude. It also requires relevant experience in the area one is seeking to make a career in. Many organisations have stringent recruitment processes, while others have more relaxed ones. Many industries such as educational institutions, banking, financial firms focus on certifications or scores based on entrance tests, whereas some are content even if the candidate is only a graduate. Many organisations have moved to psychometric testing, while some have online tests based on situation handling. No matter how advanced an organisation may be in its recruitment process, the element of **'trust'** becomes the key surviving factor for any employee. People with little or no credibility may pave their way to the top but usually do not survive. This is because **'trust'** is the most important factor in a relationship. Whether personal or professional, honesty and integrity are traits that make you an unbiased and admired human being.

In the modern technological era, artificial intelligence has also substituted many roles in industries such as airlines, hospitality, insurance and banking, to name a few. This has helped companies not only reduce employee costs but also have an error-free work pattern which is otherwise human-dependent. The banking system too has advanced to an extent that one does not have to leave their homes to even make a fixed deposit. There are no signatures involved once your account is successfully opened. Today everything is available at the click of a button from the comfort of one's home. Not many years ago, home deliveries were a challenge and were restricted to certain items as they could be procured only through a courier. However, today there has been a 360-degree revolution and everything from groceries to cooked meals, desserts, apparel, electronics and anything else that one can think of is available at the doorstep. Companies like Amazon have forayed into e-commerce, followed by many others, including food delivery chains. Many weddings are the outcome of on line meeting, dating and marriage portals.

Technology has advanced to an unbelievable level and is growing even faster than 'a blink of an eye.' Today one does not need to be physically present in office to mark one's attendance or apply for leave. Every call that is made into and out of an organisation can be monitored and traced. Reports can be generated remotely. Companies have moved to cloud-based software that can be accessed from anywhere. We have gone paperless in our administration and saved many trees. Today's 'Gen Alpha' is not comfortable with paperwork. Their mobiles are their offices, which they can easily carry with them everywhere they go. Parents can no longer discuss work with their kids as the generation gap simply cannot be matched. Technology has made school children even more competent than their parents or adults who were born in the 1980s. Apps and social media have multiple engagement features which adults could have only learnt through special tutorials, coaching and more annoyingly, their children.

The very simple conclusion derived out of all this is that technology is rapidly changing and that it is the way forward. People who do not adapt will perish. No matter which generation you belong to, if you plan on working or being self-employed, one has to make sufficient investment in the right technology not just financially but intellectually as well. Competencies have to be developed to handle the requirements of the modern business world, which today has become so easily accessible.

I remember as a child, I used to be so intrigued with Captain Kirk in *Star Trek* and the USS *Enterprise*. This fancy ship could circle around the universe and Scotty (chief engineer) could transport people to another place by using the phrase 'Beam me up, Scotty'. James Bond had cars that could shoot, were aquatic and were driverless. Batman could fly and had a hi-tech bat mobile. All these super, unnatural performances that we watched in the 1980s have all become a reality today. Yes, we cannot be 'beamed up', yet people can see us at any time they choose through video apps or 3D. Isn't that simply marvellous? It's not magic, its technology. None of the super heroes that we saw went to office every day. They operated remotely, some out of their own homes and were indeed successful. They saved the world because they had technology that could support their high-speed travel, their computers and their extraordinary devices. So the bottom line here is, the sooner we accept and adapt to technology, the faster we achieve our goals. It doesn't matter from **'where'**. The only thing that matters is **'how'**.

2

Necessity is the Mother of All Inventions

With the COVID-19 pandemic making world headlines by early 2020, employers had difficult decisions to make. Initially, they began differing meetings and conferences, avoiding social gatherings and putting travel on hold. Soon after the twenty-one-day lockdown was announced in India commencing 25 March 2020, industries shut down and people were compelled to stay home. At the beginning of the lockdown, many believed that life would soon get back to normal. Unfortunately, on the announcement of the lockdown extension, organisations realised that they would have no choice but to encourage work from home to facilitate business and keep things together. Strategizing meant having human and technological intervention and no technology can be successful if it is not driven by humans. In most cases, people working at the line or operations level such as hotel staff, catering or flight attendants, pilots, factory workers, sales personnel, etc. had literally no work to perform as the nature of their job meant working from the shop floor or meeting clients. Organisations had to accept and swallow this bitter fact, but as far as the administrative and management level employees were concerned, remote working was slowly becoming a reality.

By day 15 of the lockdown, companies realised that the lockdown was spanning into extension mode and that they had to now come up with techniques and methods to keep people productively engaged as many employees were considering this period to be a paid holiday. All types of social media–based humour on the difference of 'work from home' and 'work at home' started emerging. This raised the eyebrows of the corporate world and they began working on methods and measures of initiating a Work From Home culture. Hence, the Work From Home concept originated in India and slowly turned out as the 'new work normal'.

What is this **'New Normal'** and why is it new? Well, to me, it is not new at all. I've known stories of successful entrepreneurs and executives who built business empires out of their homes. We all know that Bill Gates and Steve Jobs started businesses out of their garages. Mathematician Anand Kumar also started his IIT coaching classes (Super 30) from a tiny, dilapidated shed. Karsanbhai Patel (promoter of Nirma washing powder) started an after-office business by making and selling washing powder on his cycle door to door.

These are just a few examples of success stories that were initiated from home.

Research has shown that many countries especially the United States had initiated a Work From Home concept long over a decade ago especially for software and consulting jobs. It slowly trickled down to sales and marketing, head hunting, lawyers, charted accountants, analytics, real estate, travel and tourism, corporate social responsibility, management and leadership roles.

What Qualified Jobs for Remote Working in the Early Days

1. These jobs could be accomplished from any desk in any time zone.
2. Technology and software were already available to support these functions whether people came to office, worked from home or met clients at restaurants, cafes and other social venues.
3. Many of these jobs had hectic travel schedules either domestically or internationally and reporting to office just to mark one's attendance made no sense.
4. In smaller towns and cities, sales teams were either a one man's show or had a bunch of people who were out in the field. Companies realised that they were wasting their money on exorbitant rents just to maintain their checks and balances on people in person while this

could be done even virtually or through certain apps.

5. Data handling, analysis, tele calling and certain marketing functions were all back-end functions, where individuals performing these roles never came in customer contact, hence could be performed from any city, region or country by hiring the best talent across geographical territories for the role.

All these factors gave rise to DIVERSITY in an organisation, which, in turn, had multiple benefits.

3

Work From Home brings in Diversity

P ut very simply, diversity in the workplace means that a company hires a wide range of diverse individuals. Diversity is often misconceived as solely multicultural matters, however, it also applies to diversity of gender, race, ethnicity, age, sexuality, language, educational background and so on. But in today's society, workplace diversity doesn't just extend to hiring diverse individuals but also making sure that the participation of these employees is equal.

In today's spectrum, diversity includes the specially abled, people from economically backward classes, people across all age groups, gender/transgenders, geographies and communities without creating reservations. It is generally observed that there is a social stigma attached to recruitment of transgenders, acid attack victims or single unmarried mothers and these groups may not be included in the diversity plan of many companies.

Diversity also includes affirmative action and equal employment opportunity.

Diversity, when made part of the company culture, can provide both tangible and intangible benefits to the organisation:

1. For example, employing workers with multi -cultural and language skills can lead to a greater outreach, which helps in 'ease of doing business' within and outside the geographies that the company operates within.

2. Diversity leads to reducing social economic differences in the society, inequalities and poverty and accelerating the economic growth of communities.

3. Diversity experts believe that heterogeneous groups can contribute more creative ideas to the mix and give businesses a competitive edge.

4. Employing more women in the workplace can be a game changer. Their emotional intelligence, passion and helpful nature helps create a healthy workplace relationship and a well-rounded workforce. They have lesser egos and conflicts, are able to multitask and can maintain a better work-life balance.

5. Employing the physically challenged whether within the office or at a call centre located at the other end of the world or a tele calling job from

home can bring in financial stability, thereby supporting livelihoods.

6.   Boardroom and leadership diversity is the result of an exceptional search and recruitment process by well-managed organisations. Decision-making by the board affects business and beyond. Being able to listen to and acknowledge multiple opinions from individuals with different backgrounds, experiences and perspectives helps good corporate decision-making.

Overall, workplace diversity can have a positive impact on your workforce, customers and the community at large.

Although diversity and inclusivity is gaining momentum, it needs to be inculcated by organisations at the leadership levels. This also means creating flexible, virtual and technology-enabled workplaces. It would consist of multiple leave and holiday patterns, creating specialised infrastructure facilities, offering sabbaticals, relaxed human resource policies, etc. Although many organisations have a sabbatical policy for mothers returning to work after having children, there are still many organisations that do not have such policies in place apart from the Maternity Leave benefit Act provided by the government. Company core values will need to shift focus primarily on integrity, trust, teamwork, empathy, ethics, innovation and good Karma.

4

Industry Outlook about Work from Home Pre–COVID-19

Work from home was coexistent with office working even before COVID-19 but was never accepted in totality. Most people who worked from home were not employees on payroll and worked as consultants or retainers. Many compromised on the compensation and benefit packages. Many women left their full-day jobs and took a 50 percent pay cut to continue the same job from home for half a day. So although this form of work existed, it was never something to be proud of as employers were in denial of this work form being performed successfully and accepted professionally.

On the other hand, for smaller businesses and start-ups, it was the only option available as one could not invest in hefty office spaces and still have a presence in both A and B category cities. With technology advancing and 4G foraying in the country, uninterrupted internet connections even in the remotest of villages became possible. Video calling through WhatsApp and Skype started gaining popularity in the year 2015–2016 and start-ups started pan India recruitment through remote working.

Work from home or remote working cannot be implemented for all job functions. There are some core operational jobs which cannot be executed unless one is on the shop floor. Many are labour intensive and customer interactive, which include face-to-face contact. One should never try to believe that all jobs can be handled remotely. That will be a predicament.

Instead, it will be important to identify all jobs that can be performed by working remotely and make them a standard practice with guidelines, technology and remote monitoring systems to ensure productivity is at its peak.

Most large MNCs or even MSMEs today have certain set of values and ethics in their Dharma. They would impact the lives of millions phenomenally if they put remote working into practice. Statistics show that 2.2 percent of the Indian population is disabled, 5 lakh are transgenders, 40 million people live below poverty line and 11.4 percent are educated unemployed. If we convert all these into numbers, we are talking about a sizeable population of the 1.5 billion people who live in this country. Through technology and remote working, we can create jobs for millions. We don't always need to brace them through corporate social responsibility but can always support them through training and skill development that will make them employable and economically stable, adding to sustainable livelihoods.

Although diversity has brought in acceptability of people, it needs to go a long way. A lot of jobs for the physically challenged can be created from the comforts of their home. These could include telesales, tele calling, marketing, information technology, research, analytics, banking and stockbroking, to name a few. There is a 'taboo' attached to employing transgenders in our society and this mind set will take years to diminish. However, we can make a start by employing them in Work From Home jobs.

Many women who are uneducated can be trained to become tailors, cooks, helpers, artists, etc. They can create products working from home and their products can still be made available in the market. Organisations like Fab India have made this happen. If such organisations had created only a factory culture, they would be generating employment limited to the community or region they operate within and their products would never have had that super touch of Incredible India. Fab India has brought local artists together through different channels by selling their products under one roof through e-commerce and retail stores. Although these people work remotely, they work for 'a multinational organisation'.

You may debate that this is an exceptional case, but that's not true. There are dozens of such examples worldwide that create job opportunities for women and marginalised sections of the society from the comfort of their villages or even their homes.

It is only when COVID-19 hit the industry that leaders started paying work from home a serious thought. Companies had no choice but to get productivity out of people who were under lockdown and thus, it not only gained acceptance but also picked up momentum. Today it has become universally accepted and is perhaps here to stay.

Now that we have seen how work from home can bring in a diverse workforce with multiple benefits, let's look at how work from home can be 'here to stay' and move way beyond the industries or profiles that have been mentioned in the introduction.

The great management guru Maslow created a pyramid which is commonly referred to as Maslow's hierarchy of needs. The bottom of the pyramid depicts the very basic needs of human beings and the top of the pyramid showcases 'self-actualisation'. How many of us in real life believe we have achieved 'self-actualisation'? What does this 'self-actualisation mean'? It does not refer to earning loads of money or owning successful businesses, becoming CEO or having tons of fame. It is a state of mind that generates personal happiness which very few people in the world can proclaim they have achieved. It eliminates stress of competition, fears, criticism and other negative energies. It is a state of contentment and spirituality in life that no money or power can buy.

We don't have to pass the point of being super rich to reach this point of self-actualisation. All we have to do is pave our way towards emotional and mental satisfaction that makes one feel successful or gives one a sense of achievement irrespective of financial or public achievements. All this is possible from the comfort of one's own home provided, of course, they put in their 100 percent towards their goals. People at office generally begin their careers from a small office workstation, move to a cubicle and then get elevated to a fancy cabin. The cabin very soon becomes substandard because a colleague has even a larger one with a better view. Then there is competition on what brand of clothes, handbags, shoes and wallets peers buy, even the pen they carry or the car they drive or are driven to work by. Hey, aren't we forgetting the fancy mobile phone, ear pods or smartwatches that are also included in our envy list? When we are not at work and are socialising, we still compete with others when we choose the restaurants we dine in and the brands of alcohol we raise our toasts to. Post that there are holidays that we take no matter how much it may pinch our pockets with a mental compulsion of advertising them to the world on social media to show off 'déjà vu', you know, 'been there done that before' kind of thing. The rat race continues with some being able to sustain it and with the others failing, being drowned in bad debts and paying ridiculously high EMIs for all the expenses incurred on keeping the competition alive.

Before we discuss this competitive world any further in the business context, let me take you through a tale of a young woman who believes she has achieved 'self-actualisation' through remote working and without having to go through any of the above. This is not because she was extraordinary or was born with a golden spoon; it is because of what she chose in life and stood by those choices.

5

Meet Meghan

Ladies and gentlemen, meet Meghan, an intelligent woman whom I know and who is now a successful executive in one of the leading companies in corporate India.

Meghan was a school-topper and an all-round student. Be it academics, singing, dancing, sports, elocutions, debates, Meghan had topped them all. Post completing her school, she graduated in commerce with management and mass communication as majors. She completed her master's in business management with majors in human resources management and minors in marketing twenty years ago from the state university that she was brought up in. Meghan was into this rushed race of finishing her education and did not stop to look back and decide whether management was even her cup of tea. Her mind was overpowered by parental, family and peer pressures to study further so that she could get a great job in life.

Meghan completed her master's with flying colours and was selected in her first campus interview. She had no real time to research or decide the sector or type of organisation she wanted to work for. The idea was to take what came along with a good salary package topped with a big brand. With a sister who came from a hospitality background, Meghan was always intrigued with the stories and gossip that she heard about the industry. Also wanting to continue living in her hometown, she decided to take up a job in hospitality and got selected by a large international chain of hotels as assistant manager in human resources.

Meghan is great at marketing, a good content writer and a fancy orator. However, twenty years ago, marketing meant taking up a field job, it was not backed by technology and the digital marketing era was non-existent. Individuals had to go out and meet clients and then come back to the office while they sat at desktops to complete their reports. Laptops were a luxury and Android technology did not exist, leave aside marketing apps. Meghan decided to save her skin from being beaten by the brutal heat and pollution of this big bad world and ventured into human resources, which happened to be a desk job. No regrets about that as this emerged to be the stepping-stone of her success story.

Let me warn you that Meghan is no CEO, CXO, celebrity or millionaire. Meghan is a woman who believes she has achieved 'self-actualisation' – the topmost part of the Maslow's pyramid – by being who she chose to be.

Meghan is best described as loving, caring, creative, energetic, giving, forgiving, intelligent, passionate, honest, exploring and most of all, a stickler for perfection. The traits that make her every other woman's envy is that she is independent – **mentally, physically and spiritually**. No one can tell Meghan what to do, where to go or how to live her life. That does not mean that she lives only out of her selfish free will and will not oblige others. Meghan is like the mixed box of candies that only makes you feel good. Just as a candy box has candies in different shapes, colours, texture, it also has candies with varied proportions of sugar, some of which are even made of dark chocolate or are sugar-free. All I am trying to point out here is that Meghan has mixed qualities and talents. She can deliver positive outcomes to people and projects through the bittersweet side of her. She is one of those who is brave enough to tell you that she doesn't agree, bold enough to give you negative feedback and most of all, apologise in case she makes mistakes. Someone who has no ego, says please and thank you during every conversation and treats people with care and dignity. Let me also tell you that she is happily married and a mother of a gorgeous 13-year-old.

I'm hoping many of you reading this book will relate Meghan to either yourselves, your mothers, friends or certain role models in your lives as there is a little bit of Meghan in all of us.

Meghan's first assignment was at a fancy luxury hotel chain, where she played a role in human resources. This was the first time Meghan moved out of home and started living all by herself except for the two years where she had spent in a hostel while pursuing her master's. Work and travel put together consumed thirteen hours of her day and certain site visits by her directors even consumed her Sundays. However, she always claims that the learning was immense and the team bonding was memorable since it was a pre-opening hotel. The greatest learning was to be flexible, be attentive, anticipate, accept, delight and cope up with long working hours that freshers had no clue about whatsoever. I am certain most hoteliers will be able to connect to this lifestyle as 90 percent of them live this way. When a hotelier returns back home after a long day, they have no time for family, not even a meal. Their kids are already in bed and they find themselves eating out of the fridge, watching that idiot box all alone. They have many vices and have little or no energy. Singles generally party almost every night, smoke, drink and get about five to six hours of sleep if they are lucky. They try hard to get an afterwork life, where they can let down their hair as their job mainly deals with keeping others not just happy but also delighted. The stress and fatigue levels are very high as a hotelier has to play the role of an actor on a stage for over twelve hours a day.

Meghan did feel the same at times, but since this was her first assignment, she did not want to give up. She wanted to learn to cope up and deal with situations and work pressures until, alas, a tragic incident forced her to change her decision.

One afternoon, Meghan decided to hitch a ride on her way home with a colleague on his bike. While on the road, they were hit by an oncoming truck and were dragged along the roadside. Meghan thanked GOD for keeping her alive as she believed that she would not make it. Lucky to have a doctor and ambulance service nearby, Meghan and her colleague were rushed to the hospital, where they were treated. However, the accident put Meghan's leg in a cask for a whole month. She had no movement in her toes and had to learn to walk all over again. This reduced her ability to travel as she had to travel two hours each day to get to work. Hence, Meghan was forced to move to her second job, where travel was less, which she did out of no choice.

In her second assignment, she handled 'personnel management', the old-fashioned term used for human resources that we do not hear of much today. She was dealing with tough union and labour issues, which taught her good negotiating skills and at the same time, gave her hands on experience about labour laws. She would deal with labour tribunals, commissioners, lawyers and the police with ease even at a tender age of 23 years.

When Meghan had enough of all this and was threatened with her life by some union members, she decided to move on rather than have a security guard escort her home every day, a memory that is still fresh in her mind even today.

Meghan then moved on to heading human resources for two hotels in one of India's biggest hotel chains. She claims that this was her greatest learning and helped her percolate into a leadership role. The work hours were crazy and thus, Meghan moved out of home, just five minutes away from the hotel, but worked twelve hours every day. Here, she learnt strategy, decision-making, union handling, training and development, guest relations apart from all the human resource functions that were available in an ideal job description. She travelled to many places and because of her creativity and content skills, was made the process owner for a specialised recruitment programme and an employee connect magazine.

Meghan worked really hard day and night not because she was forced to but because the challenges that came to her because of this role were truly fulfilling. The long hours didn't seem endlessly long to her. She would work at least two Sundays a month. She made many friends at work and they caught up every night at one or the others homes, ate dinner, sang and drank together. The bonding was so strong and positive that Meghan and the gang cherish those memories even today although miles apart.

6

The Love of Her Life

It was during this time that Meghan met the love of her life, a tall, handsome and superbly intelligent lad who stole her heart instantly. It was indeed love at first sight and they tied the knot within six months of courtship. They came from two different states and two different religions, thus different thought processes and cultures. While the Catholic wedding was all about meat and wine, the Hindu wedding was entirely vegetarian with soft beverages. Meghan wondered how she would cope up with such a different culture, but it was meant to be and the two of them took a strong decision to never let their families or cultures come in the way of their relationship.

Meghan is an extrovert and loves singing, dancing and travelling. She loves cars and heading out on long drives with her favourite music playing. On the other hand, Meghan's husband, Anand, is calm, composed, patient and extremely mature. Anand is an individual who stands his grounds, never shows off his high IQ, is a firm believer of God and always keeps the balance in the relationship. Meghan gives him huge credit for whatever she is today. Very few women get unprecedented spouse support to accomplish their dreams. Very few women can live their lives like free birds after marriage. A very possessive husband with a heart of gold, Meghan knew that she had made the best decision of her life, something that she was very thankful to God for. Both families bonded extremely well over time. Meghan and Anand lived away from their parents, but their parents on both sides of the family were extremely supportive.

Meghan came from a middle-class family with working parents. Her parents had senior positions in the government. Meghan always watched her mother strike a balance between work and her three children. Times were different when Meghan was growing up. Infrastructure and technology was not as advanced, but yet Meghan always saw her mother as **'superwoman'**, being able to handle everything like a piece of cake without losing her temper. She would wake up early morning, make breakfast, pack lunch boxes for the kids, make sure they never missed the school bus, make lunch and then leave for work. She would get back home by 6.30 p.m. and then cook dinner for the family. She sometimes helped them with their homework. She had her weekends free, that gave the family ample time to bond.

Meghan's dad would generally take both Meghan and her sister to sports camps and often to the club, where they played table tennis and Badminton. He was instrumental in them achieving many medals and accolades. Meghan expresses gratitude towards her family. She proclaims to have been born in the best family one could ever have and would not have it any other way. She attributes her strengths to her mother. 'The most important learning from my mother was *being independent*,' says Meghan. This did not mean being single or selfish or ignoring other people's ideas and sentiments. It meant being self-reliant, emotionally and financially and not blaming the world or circumstances for your failures. Becoming independent takes a lot of perseverance and patience. At times, it even means being thick-skinned or giving up things that mean the most to you. It is only one life that we have and if we want to feel that it has been meaningful, then we must be ready to handle disappointments, criticism as well as stardom.

A few months before the wedding, Meghan moved to head human resources for another company. She never wanted her relationship to ever come in the way of work. Neither did she want to become the gossip centre while she and Anand were dating. Being in the role of human resources, she didn't want her personal life to draw attention at work. Both Meghan and Anand were heading departments and had positions of responsibility, hence, Meghan decided to take up another exciting hotel assignment. Within a few months of being married and into a new job, Meghan realised that they were expecting a baby and had to take some tough decisions, which would impact her life long term.

7

Taking Tough Decisions

All of us at some juncture or the other have battled decisions that have either rocked our careers or made them stall. The choice is always open and I would recommend everyone to have a balanced approach where one can weigh the pros and cons before they take a final decision. Also, once decided, there should be no regrets no matter what the consequences are. People should also be bold enough to come out of a bad decision or situation rather than carry this baggage and regret it all their lives.

For those of you who are wondering what Meghan did, well, she decided to quit and become a mother. She used to self-drive to work for forty-five minutes every day. Considering the pregnancy and major back injuries out of the old accident, Meghan decided to put health first. If Meghan worked in today's age and world, quitting may not have been the decision she would be forced to take. She could have got pre-delivery maternity leave, been able to take a sabbatical or even work out of home, but unfortunately, times were different then.

Quitting was hard and when one works nine to ten hours a day, suddenly having nothing to do makes life seem empty. One feels let down as all the effort and hardships one had sailed through suddenly become meaningless. Meghan, however, took it with a pinch of salt and decided to focus on her health and the baby. While she was home trying to recover from her badly wounded back with four ligament tears, she was pleasantly surprised by a few phone calls that brightened up her life and took away the disappointment that she was going through. Described as loving and of a helpful nature earlier, Meghan started getting calls from educational institutions with Deans requesting her to teach human resource management to graduate and postgraduate students. This she could do on a daily or hourly basis. She could still continue all the other things from home that she loved doing and simultaneously have enough time to focus on physiotherapy and recovery. Meghan was able to take time off for her delivery, spend time with her students by going to college for a few hours a week and many of them even came home for extra classes and inputs. This was a turning point in Meghan's life, where she realised that she could work wonders by working from home and she made it *The New Normal in her life way back in the year 2007.*

"I was motivated to tell the world about my experience and how I have been working remotely for thirteen years", says Meghan. COVID-19 or not, with the advent of technology, integrity and good interpersonal skills, one can **'pave the highway to success from home'**. If one does all the right things at the right time and in the right way, the world can be at your fingertips. However, integrity is the most critical personal trait and the rest depends on flexibility and multitasking.

8

The New 'start up'- A consulting firm

Once the baby was six months old, Meghan took a decision to start her own consulting firm in partnership with two of her closest friends. The first and most expensive investment made in the business was a laptop at Rs. 65,000/-. This was procured out of the bonus Anand had earned. He was more than happy to give it to her and this is where it all began. Her other two partners handled the banking clients and looked after admin and accounts. The first step began with finding a name for the company, registering it and opening a bank account. The next was developing a website, followed by hiring associates and marketing the company. Start-ups cannot afford to hire just anyone. They have to recruit diligently and ensure that these people can enhance the reputation of the organisation. Hence, the company was very careful on who the first hire was.

Meghan pulled out her entire contact list that she had made while in the industry. She took appointments from human resource professionals and company owners. She met them with illuminating presentations. She won many contracts through her experience and relationship management skills. Let me reiterate that social media had still not entered the Indian market in 2007 and neither were smart phones available, hence, marketing was an expensive medium as most organisations relied on print and phone marketing. Outgoing calls were charged at pretty high rates way back then unlike today and rentals were extremely high. The internet network was slow and dongles had just started emerging.

Few months after Meghan had launched the business, Anand had to move to another state because of his job. This job was important to him and Meghan again had tough decisions to make. She had worked really hard to set up the business, make it popular and now as things were finally settling down, she saw herself being unsettled again. She knew that if she wanted to keep the relationship going and Stephanie to have her father while growing up, she would have to come up with a ridiculously great solution.

9

Building a Remote Working Culture

With a 6-month-old infant, Meghan decided to join Anand. One thing she knew for certain is that 'family comes first'. She had always seen her parents stay together no matter how difficult situations were and how her father had refused promotions just to be with the family. However, this migration to another city did not put her on the back foot but rather taught her to find ways of moving forward. While her partners stayed back to manage the show in her home state, Meghan moved house and started working from home, servicing a pan India market. She moved with Anand and set up an office at their new home. She took a decision to carry on working and servicing all her clients from the new city, even if she had to fly to meet them. She would talk to them often, meet them at least twice a year, send them birthday wishes and Christmas gifts. She very clearly built relationships way beyond business and friendships that would last a lifetime.

Meghan hired associates across different states who possessed high integrity through interrogative and superior interview handling techniques and ensured they were tech-savvy. She treated them like extended family and was very pally even with their parents and boyfriends.

Most of Meghan's hires were women because she believed that women possess certain soft skills that men don't and that they have higher integrity levels, are multitasked and have lesser vices than men. Also, since most of the jobs got done over the phone, it was observed that a woman's voice was more acceptable than a male counterpart. Fewer number of calls would be dropped or rejected if a lady with a smart, pleasant voice initiated a sales call. After three months of handholding the associates in their jobs, Meghan allowed them to work from the comfort of their homes on the condition that they would answer all calls and emails promptly.

Those who worked in the same city reported once a week and those in other cities reported through Skype and phone calls. Virtual morning meetings were conducted daily and apart from all the professional data being shared, the team exchanged jokes, grandmother recipes and tales, their best and worst habits and even family pictures. Those living in the same city often came together for potluck and dance parties. In this way, the team demographics widened and remote working that was little heard of became a reality.

Meghan's associates interacted with one another through various mediums and shared fabulous relationships with one another, although many had not met in person or over social media as social media was non-prevalent during those days. They had to trust one another's capabilities and build relationships so that they could work together. Some of them even worked for three years without meeting one another. Meghan had almost zero percent attrition. Yes, she might have fired two to three people in her entire career with the consulting firm, but those were so because they weren't honest to their work and were not able to meet the company's goals. However, the firm did follow certain procedures before they took a decision to terminate.

Stages in the Termination Process

1. Adequate counselling and advice was given to people before they were asked to leave.
2. Weaknesses were clearly discussed and methods to improve on the same were shared.
3. Warning letters were placed on the files in case three advisories were ineffective.
4. Termination letter was issued only as a last resort, after giving sufficient time for improvement.

Fortunately, even people who were terminated are still in touch with Meghan even when I interviewed her to write this book and were great fans of hers. When I asked Meghan how difficult it is to fire someone, she says,

Firing someone is a horrible thing to do. It's mentally and emotionally disturbing even if you know that they were guilty. However, there are some things you have to do to ensure that you comply with organisational ethics and policies and also so that you don't create an open playground for foul play. Our organisation was built around freedom and trust. Our permanent registered office was open only one day a week. We created a structure that would offer flexibility to individuals but would not compromise on discipline and core values. It respected people's privacy, personal and family time. Hence, in return, we would expect 100 percent commitment from our associates.

10

A Glimpse of the Flexible Working Structure

Meghan, narrates

Office hours (Work from Home) began at 9 a.m. for some and 10 am for others. Everyone worked a nine-hour shift. During this time, we expected people to completely dedicate themselves towards work no matter whether they were working from home or choose to come to office, which could even mean coming to my house. We did not mark their attendance. However, we wanted to be rest assured that they would log in and out in time. Many people had to help out in regular household chores like pay electricity bills or take their parents grocery shopping. In this case, they were to inform their supervisors in advance and make up for the time lost by adding in extra hours. They would also request their colleagues to cover up for their shift so that there would be no loss of revenue.

We were in the consulting business and time was money for us. At times, we would lose a talent acquisition function to another head hunter by under a minute and therefore, if we decided to take time off, we would require our colleagues to cover our back. In this manner, we were able to build excellent relationships within the company and ensure we did not lose out on business.

However, those who could not adhere to these guidelines had no space in our organisation. The flaw here could be that we had not recruited the right candidate or that some people cannot adapt to a Work From Home environment. They are not as disciplined at home. Only offices can discipline them and they need constant supervision. The culture that we built was one free from supervision. Each person was responsible for the targets set and had to achieve them. We never fired people if they were short of achieving their targets but counselled and trained them on methods to achieve goals.

We always nurtured people with good character, values and attitude as we believed that these people with the right inputs from our end could take the company to even greater heights.

Organisational Structure

The organisational structure was flat with associates reporting directly to Meghan and her partners. At a given time, Meghan would have four to five associates reporting to her alone. On completion of targets and two years of service, the associates were usually promoted.

Compensation Structure

The consulting firm had a structure of fixed and variable pay. The fixed pay was the monthly salary and the flexible pay consisted of the following:

1. Bonus paid on achievement of KRAs
2. Phone and internet reimbursements
3. Meal allowance
4. Fuel reimbursement

Recruitment, Induction and Training

The recruitment, induction and subsequent training programmes ensured that the following were covered:

1. Core values
2. Market Analysis (hospitality, information technology, engineering, mining and education)
3. Client list
4. Communication skills
5. Social skills
6. Customer relationship management
7. Response management
8. Management information systems reports
9. Weekly industry updates

Again reiterating, in those days where there were no social media channels available, being in the headhunting profession was very difficult. It relied on cold-calling or getting in touch with candidates who came through referrals or advertisements. The quality of profiles were average and the only way of connecting with a person's face was to rely on a passport-sized photograph which wasn't enough to gauge a candidate's personality. Hence they ended up relying on their instincts most of the time.

LinkedIn had just stepped in and Facebook and Twitter, although just launched, had not gained momentum as most people were still using Blackberrys or Nokias that offered only text messaging. Android phones got introduced to India in 2008, were then expensive and the internet speed was still in the 2G mode.

Surprising for millennials to digest all this but so true.

Keeping all of the above in mind, associates relied on building relationships and strong networks through references and other associates. The business flourished across states as associates worked from home from different parts of the country and grew the business in their regions. Revenues grew, everyone got paid in time and the firm became one of the most preferred consulting firms in the country. Meghan and partners were earning twice as much as they would have in a regular management job and had a great 'work-life balance'.

11

The Key to Employer– Employee Happiness

All of the above is an ideal outcome of remote working. A happy and productive team, flexibility, competitive compensation and a great work-life balance can increase the happiness quotient of employees. Also, timely and quality delivery of services, zero customer complaints, excellent interpersonal and PR skills with clients raise the goodwill of a company, enhancing its brand reputation.

One must remember that no business whether from home or from office can be successful without good interpersonal and customer handling skills. The customer is the king and satisfying customers is indeed a challenge. Many new recruits who joined out of campus had great communication skills but not necessarily the right interactive or customer-centric skills. Many struggled to handle assignments independently. Customers would want to talk only to the promoters if they had special requests, but the consulting firm continued to handhold its associates by imbibing the necessary techniques and eventually made them capable of handling even the most difficult customer.

In the corporate world, it is evident that if the big boss is looped in on a project, the job gets 100 percent done, but the consulting firm wanted its associates to break out of this ritual and believed that if two people sit across a table for discussion, they are on an equal platform. Trust and confidence should not be undermining factors but the most critical factors in a negotiation. They wanted associates to become confident and deal with customers rather than have a superior intervene at all times.

When employees are trained well, are trusted and are empowered, they will give their best. Meghan would encourage associates to meet clients and take up new projects even in areas they had not worked in before. She did this after evaluating the strengths of individuals. She understood that job enrichment was a very crucial factor in achieving career growth. Apart from delivering regular assignments, the associates were involved in billing, accounting, taxation and even recoveries. Transparency in day-to-day operations was indeed motivating. They were taught to take complete onus for a project, right from pitching for it until the payment phase. At times, this process took up to three months, but patience coupled with performance mapping and relationship management was the most critical part for the consulting firm. If these principles were abided by, money would be no constraint for the firm or for its employees.

12

A Dilemma for the Second Time

After having spent six years with the consulting firm, a large assignment came by through a known gentleman whose vision was to start a new hospitality chain. The assignment was indeed alluring and Meghan did not think twice before taking it up as part of the consulting firm. The assignment was challenging as it involved incorporating some of the best practices in human resources and operations. The company was seeking to be the best in the hospitality Industry in India in the midmarket segment through a unique Karmic vision, which did feel strange when Meghan initially accepted the assignment. All start-ups must relate to the communities they operate within and look after their well-being to be successful. Goodwill cannot be compromised on any accord. Meghan decided to visit the site where construction was to commence. She wanted to understand for herself what she was getting into. She had to get a feel of the product and the place, understand the pricing and positioning, very frequently referred as the 4 Ps of marketing. Setting up an industry in rural India was a huge task and it being hospitality was even more challenging.

Requirements for a Successful Start-Up

1. Product knowledge
2. Customer Centricity
3. Competitor mapping
4. Talent pool of human resources
5. Strong processes
6. Supplier network
7. Hi-tech information systems
8. Sound financial planning
9. Marketing strategy
10. Legal, advisory and liaising with local authorities
11. Competent and efficient sales and marketing workforce
12. Strong community network

While setting up a company, the local community and government are of core significance as one has to operate within the jurisdiction of that competent authority. Secondly, every community welcomes new businesses when they see a direct as well as an indirect benefit to them. This could be in terms of employment, supplier networks, contracting jobs, corporate social responsibility, etc. The moment this connection is formed between the organisation and the locals, rest assured you can set up successfully.

The site visit was indeed enduring. Meghan got a first-hand experience of what rural India looked like. She saw poverty, hospitals that looked more like nursing homes that were badly maintained, schools that had insufficient classrooms, no washrooms or drinking water, no local transport system available, people spoke only the local language, women worked in fields to put food on the table, girls who were not allowed to go to school and nobody who ventured out into the street beyond 6 p.m.

On the other hand, she saw beautiful sugarcane and pomegranate farms, grapevines, local cattle farms, bullock carts and ploughs, herds of sheep, clear blue skies and windmills. She breathed absolutely pure air and could hear the chirping of exotic birds all day long. She felt one with nature and fell in love with the place. The place, although situated in an industrial belt, had loads to offer beyond just corporate hotel rooms.

Meghan knew the task was cumbersome, but she was never judgemental about any of the facts that she encountered. She started working with the local community and a set of recruiters to create a diverse workforce which would blend into the hotel and eventually form a warm and caring culture that would create memories for its guests.

13

The New BOSS

Meghan was 'SOLD' to the vision of the managing director, Narayan, who had a vision like no other person she had ever met before. He wanted to build a family that would last way beyond brick and motor, a family that was diverse, loving, respectful, helpful with high credibility and no compromise on efficiency. He was a man who did not care where you worked from, who treated you with respect, told you about his flaws and weaknesses without fumbling, who was transparent, motivating and encouraging. He was a man who rewarded you with a big hug, shared your every success with his family and even spoke to your spouse, praising every good thing you did. He would tell you on your face when he agreed and when he didn't, when he was upset or dissatisfied. This led to Meghan improving her efficacy by leaps and bounds. This gentleman looked beyond the Profit and Loss account, beyond the consulting contract Meghan had with him. He never intervened during her family time, understood when she called in sick, wished her a speedy recovery and even offered to courier her medicines if they were unavailable. He treated people like his very own, like he had worked with them for decades. He told Meghan he wanted to build an institution, but she felt like he was developing a little country within a gigantic one, a country that was self-sufficient, educated, employable, had a good produce and could afford three meals a day for the family. Meghan was now beginning to see the vision become a reality.

This was for the first time she had experienced such unique leadership qualities in an individual that went way beyond management books and theories. She worked remotely on finding the best processes, practices and people and travelled once in every three months to the site, which was a two-hour flight and then a six-hour drive. She stayed in a nearby inn for over ten days at a stretch before she left back for home. She walked with farmers and their spouses visiting fields, dined at their homes, visited schools and networked with the children. She recruited women from marginalised communities, trained them and made them employable. She visited nearby villages and towns to recruit people with special abilities, which included the blind and orthopedically challenged. She also began a programme exclusively for underprivileged girls. Meghan was experiencing a different side of life, a life that brought out a different energy. After two years of remotely working on the consulting assignment, she felt that she could give much more in a corporate role rather than in a consulting role.

But why would an independent, successful young woman like Meghan leave a Work From Home role and join corporate life? Isn't that like a huge compromise? Why would she go back to the corporate rat race that she left behind years ago. Why would she deal with bureaucracy and internal politics while she was currently her own boss? What and why was her calling? Most people would have loved to be Meghan, but Meghan realised she wanted to be different. Confused? Let me explain.

14

Back to the Corporate World

After evaluating the odds, Meghan went ahead and accepted the offer. The offer was not lucrative enough for her to give up her own baby and manage someone else's. Yet Meghan chose to sell her stake in the consulting firm and moved ahead to a corporate role. She believed in being ethical and having loyalty to the new company that she was now part of and thus detached herself from the consulting firm. This was the most painful moment of Meghan's life, but her values and ethics was what made her the person she was and she knew it was the right thing to do.

While interacting with Meghan on this subject, I saw her eyes light up and even fill with tears. I was wondering if this was what she really wanted. Giving up a business while you are six years into profitability is not easy and not something most people would opt for. Then why did Meghan do this? My curiosity now rose to a different level.

Meghan explained,

> I had everything one wanted. There was
> flexibility, I worked for approximately six hours
> a day, took almost four holidays a year, had
> time for Stephanie, cooked on weekends and
> networked well in the industry. However, the
> one thing I felt I did not have was the potential
> to explore beyond the nature of my work. My
> job was satisfying and challenging, but it did not
> give me the advantage of exploring the potential
> of my inner self. I was a human resource and
> training professional. I had worked in this field
> with big brands both Indian and international.
> I had recruited people right from associate
> to general manager levels, I had travelled the
> country to train corporates on leadership and
> other self-development programmes, I advised
> companies on how to minimise their payroll
> and run an efficient compensation system, I set
> human resources standard operating procedures
> for many old businesses who were expanding or
> becoming public, I also had sufficient experience
> in labour laws, legal matters, I had handled union
> settlements and signed charters of demands. All
> these were core human resources competencies
> that I had developed and indulged into for over
> twelve years. This is what I was known for in
> the industry. This is why companies consulted
> me. Every management level recruitment

generated a 12 percent of annual gross salary as fees. Every consulting assignment was a learning by itself as I had moved way beyond hospitality and had begun to get a taste of other industries. However, my most exquisite traits of impressionable creativity, marketing, MIS and social responsibility were bottled up inside of me. It's like hiding your best features at a Venetian mask party where the crowd only sees your expressive eyes but misses out on all your other stellar features.

Frequent visits to the hotel site had changed my life and I was hoping that I could value add to others as well, be it women or children. I now wanted to give back to communities, to understand my strengths more intensely and see if I could further enhance them. Money was never a constraint. As a family, Anand and I had enough. His job earned us more than enough to have a comfortable life. However, I always wanted financial independence. This is something I learnt from my mother and I value that learning even today. I never wanted to get introduced as someone's wife. I wanted to be known independently as myself with my very own name. I am one of those women who kept my maiden name with pride and I am blessed that Anand never took it to heart. I wanted to explore myself, get out of my comfort zone and challenge the risks involved. I had some 'me time' that made me realise that life is way beyond living in our comfort zones. One had to get uncomfortable or unsettled at times to understand one's real self. Money can also bring you temporary worldly pleasures, but it cannot buy you happiness. It cannot help you connect with your spiritual self. Money is temporary and thus, one should indulge in what one can do to be happy in the long run. To me, I wanted to learn other functions. I didn't mind working twelve hours a day. Stephanie was now 6 years old and I felt that I have the flexibility to travel. I read three newspapers every morning that gave me enough general insight. I surfed on social media every day and all this gave me strength of doing something different. There were a lot of inspiring stories, industrialists, philanthropists and management gurus whom I followed and this following led me to believing that anything is possible. The world can be at your fingertips if you choose to and you don't need some fancy corner office with the best view of the city to have it all.

I wasn't sure whether I was heading back towards that rat race, but I was ready to explore. I knew that I was only adding to my experience even if it was beyond my core competency and all this would help me have a stronger industry profile if I ever wanted to start consulting again. I also knew that I was adding to my patience levels, my scope of work and working hours. I was ready to accept that all these could come to me without any rewards and without any appreciation. Yet still, I took that leap of faith and decided to get employed. I sold my share in the consulting firm for a handsome rate and I retained the company name for a price. It was of emotional value to me as I had conceptualised it myself. I had a fantastic relationship with my partners. I allowed them to use the name of the consulting firm for continuing the business without accepting any fee for the same. Who knows when I would go back and if I ever did, I would not want to start from scratch.

The company welcomed Meghan with open arms, admired her dedication and creative thinking and invited her to join them in a full-time yet flexible role. Meghan loved working with the owners and the entire team. She felt extremely passionate about everything. She felt like she built herself another home, just a larger one. She was able to create a unique culture of diversity and inclusion. The team worked very hard to contribute even to the environment. Right from the building being an environment friendly one, all necessary practices and procedures were put in place to save energy and water, increase afforestation cover, reduce plastic, etc.

Meghan was not only working with setting up human resources, but she was also working with communities, environmentalists, trainers and other professionals.

She was given a free hand in customer relationship management. She diligently performed all her duties from home and submitted all reports in time. She was handling human resources, training and consulting sitting miles away. She was now confident that not only self-employment but also a corporate role could be handled remotely, depending upon what the nature of the job is. This is possible only if people have high credibility, are passionate and take time management very seriously. Work from home wasn't living room or bedroom working. To Meghan, it meant a full-fledged office from home.

15

Ten Key Factors Essential for Remote Working

1. Have a space all to yourself.

Have a room or a cabin developed at your home which is private. Only you should have the power to access it. If you have family residing at home, make sure they knock or call you over your phone in case they need to reach you. If you do not have a private space or a study to yourself, you may choose to work from your bedroom. In such cases, ensure that your door is shut at all times and that you do not get tempted to lie down in bed and work.

Make the space meeting friendly (especially video meetings) and ensure it is noise-free at all times. Choose to have indoor plants, colour schemes and photographs that are soothing and motivating. Keep some water at your table as a reminder to keep your self hydrated.

2. Use modern technology.

While selecting your workspace, ensure that it has good phone and Wi-Fi network. Those who work remotely should be equipped with the most modern technology whether software or apps. Since a mobile phone is literally an 'office on the go' for most top-line executives, it makes sense to invest in top-line products and upgrade software and systems that will be necessary to perform remote working functions with ease. Make certain that you have two sim cards and a strong backup for Wi-Fi. A meeting should never be interrupted because of bad network. Have a good printer, copier, scanner, etc. If remote working is not backed by adequate technology, it can be frustrating for the employer, employee and customers. A slow internet connection or a laptop with a slow processor can interfere with your efficiency.

Ensure that you have an updated antivirus software. Keep your webcam shut at all times except when you are using it for video calling. Do not access emails from your spam folder unless you are certain about its safety. Contact your information technology head or your service agent in case you notice any irregularities. Take a backup of your data (an automated process by companies) or, if self-employed, ensure that you keep backups of both your email and data.

3. Have adequate ergonomics.

Your private space should have a work desk large enough to accommodate your laptop, printer, chargers, a diary and some papers. It should be dust-free and cleaned every single day before you start work. This workstation should be no different from the one that you would have in a formal office setup as it should make you feel that you are working from your office out of home. Set up your private space with adequate stationary and all the other equipment you may need without having to get up frequently. This would also include simple things like a stationery kit and a few healthy munchies.

Choose a chair that is comfortable that has arms and a good backrest. You must invest in a chair that rotates, has an adjustable height and a comfortable seat. Do not compromise on the quality of your chair as you spend more than eight hours on it. Ensure that you have sufficient lighting and ventilation. Make sure that the laptop you use has adjustable screens or install anti reflecting screens to make your life easy. Spending nine to ten hours a day can deteriorate one's eye sight, hence, never compromise on ergonomics. Invest in the best.

4. Plan and organise.

Ensure that you have planned your day the previous day itself. Follow a planner whether manually or digitally. Set priorities. Use technology that sets meeting reminders and alarms for lunch and short breaks, organise your emails and set a timetable for the day that you believe you can accomplish before you switch off. Things that remained undone because of whatever reasons, if not priorities, can be moved to the next day. It may not be possible to complete all tasks by day's end, hence, prioritising will help you achieve targets as well as give you peace of mind.

It is absolutely all right to pitch in to do family chores. If you have taken the responsibility to do the dishes or pay bills or tutor your kids, stand by your promises. To do so, you need to set your schedule right through proper planning and organising skills.

5. Have a schedule or a regime.

Do not get to your workstation in your pajamas. Make sure you exercise, brush, bathe, change, groom, pray and complete all your morning rituals before reaching your desk. If you work on a particular shift, then ensure that you are at your desk five minutes before time. People often assume that those who work from home can get straight out of bed in their PJs and get to their desk. However, this is definitely not recommended as it will never create a formal and disciplined environment.

Creating a formal environment is very crucial to achieve success while working from home. Many people who take this lightly run late to meetings end up skipping meals, eating at odd hours, working late nights all because they did not have a fixed regime. Never start work without breakfast. If you are not the early-morning-breakfast type, then have a breakfast latest by 10 a.m. Anything beyond that leads to acidity. Short breaks of five minutes and a lunch break of half an hour are extremely important to refresh the mind so that productivity is at its best. Stretch your arms and feet at regular intervals to avoid any backbone or joint-related issues.

6. Take authorised leave.

Don't be guilty or feel like a superhero because you work from home. You may need time off for personal work, when you or your family falls ill, to pay bills, go shopping and so on. If any of these do come your way, inform your bosses and apply for leave in case you are an employee. In case you are self-employed, inform your employees. In this manner, you can have your personal space during your free time and nobody will form an assumption about your character or behaviour. When you are back from leave, be on the top of things. Take updates on what you missed out on and follow up in case you had work assigned to others.

In case you don't need leave but just need a couple of hours off, I would still recommend that you get it authorised. Complete trust needs to be built with the people you work with and if you have developed this healthy and transparent relationship, rest assured that your superiors will have no issues with your style of working as they believe in your integrity.

7. Eat healthy.

Eat light, eat after short intervals and avoid fried meals and heavy desserts. All these foods, if not avoided, will set in lethargy and will cause weight issues, which will, in turn, lead you to accumulate belly fat which is difficult to burn. This can also lead to high cholesterol and blood pressure at an early age. Eat in time. The general tendency when we work from home is to eat late breakfasts and snack on anything that is available at odd hours. This should be avoided at all times. One has to create a specific diet pattern and religiously adhere to it. This diet should include loads of fruits and vegetables, light juices and water to keep oneself hydrated. Working on your laptop and phone for nine to ten hours a day can lead to fatigue and hence, it is essential to keep yourself energised and refreshed at all times by adopting the right dietary plan.

8. Set rules with the family.

You may have family – parents, spouse, children – living at home. Ensure that they do not disturb you unless absolutely necessary. Children need to be trained to understand that you are there for them at all times, but since you are at work, you need that personal space.

They need to understand that if you went to office every day, they would not have free access to you and therefore should respect your privacy. You may be physically present in the house but cannot be engulfed with their needs all the time. Teach your children to be patient and respect your privacy. This will go a long way in life and help them develop good management skills. Long-distance calls with family and friends should be limited during work hours. Ensure that you don't attend to the doorbell or house phone just because you work from home. Never leave a meeting to answer the doorbell unless absolutely necessary.

9. Stop being a perfectionist.

Remote working nowhere defines that you are a perfectionist. All superheroes have made mistakes and even taken a beating from villains, but that didn't stop them from getting up and saving the world. Don't feel like you are not being a good parent. Guilt can lead us to believing all the wrong things about ourselves. The guilt factor exists mainly in women because of the societal mind-set that women should be homemakers or only mothers. If a woman is unable to attend a parent–teacher meeting or if kids score badly in academics, women are made to feel responsible and those failures are because they do not dedicate enough time to the family. Some women sail through all this and some simply cannot. If you want to be able to cope up with such pressures, set your day right, be prepared to feel disappointed and learn to deal with frustrations. One cannot be the ideal parent, employee, sibling, spouse, house help, teacher, mentor all at the same time. Yes, these are the many hats you sport all at one time when you decide to work from home as there is no visible line that is drawn. It is 'YOU' who has to set those boundaries between work and home and you cannot be a perfectionist at every role you play. Trying to play multiple roles all at the same time can lead to burnout. Learn when to say yes and when to refuse. If you cannot handle a situation whether at work or for house chores, reach out for help. Stop pretending you are some super human being as it will lead to frustration and eventually depression.

10. Know when to switch off.

Just because you work from home doesn't mean that there is no end to your day. Align your hours of work to the timings of your superiors and subordinates. There may be times that you work long hours because of business exigencies, but do not make long hours a habit. It is not about how many hours you put in but how much productivity you put into a task. Remember the reason you are allowed to work from home is because the organisation accepts the norm and trusts you. There is no reason for superiors to question your credibility unless, of course, you have faltered many a times.

Also, many individuals find it extremely difficult to switch off. This is not just about the number of emails that come into their inbox but also about all the messaging groups one is on. Trying to be active on a messaging group or on never-ending email traffic can lead to anxiety and undue pressure. If things can wait for tomorrow, just let them wait. Being on a messaging group doesn't prove your productivity and inclusion. Know when to switch off and in case there is a fire, rest assured that you will receive a call even if it's 3 a.m. If you don't know how and when to switch off, there is no point in working from home and you might as well go to office.

Apart from all the above factors or what we call DOs and DON'Ts, there are many personal traits that one must possess to make remote working possible and successful.

16

Seven Personal Factors That Facilitate Remote Working

1. Have flexibility to the next level.

B e ready to up and travel when you have to. Don't let your gender or family become the reason for excuse. Choose a safe and reliable mode of travel, especially if you are a woman. It would be best for women to travel during daylight, use hotel cars for transfers, stay in a branded hotel that would offer more safety and security and pay the difference in case their organisations don't support such policies. Most people are hesitant to discuss these issues with their superiors, but DO NOT COMPROMISE. Organisations do understand these important issues pertaining to women's safety and are nowadays very obliging. Even if your dearness allowance is limited to a lower-category hotel or a yellow-and-black cab, make sure that you put your safety and security first. At the end of the day, it is your life that matters the most and we are all responsible for how we take care of ourselves.

Being flexible also means adapting to the need of the organisation, playing many roles simultaneously, being involved in decision-making committees and training subordinates. In other words, being able to multitask is an important trait.

If you are a manager leading a team remotely, leave all your egos and work experience behind. Be prepared to go down to the grass-root level and know every team member, their profile and, at times, even their job role. Be prepared to pitch in when people take time off no matter what level of the hierarchy you are at. Very often, people in the consulting, administration, marketing or information technology profession move so far ahead in their careers that they tend to forget where they started from or how much time and effort it took for them to reach there. They find it hard to connect with juniors or get working on a task just because they believe that they have surpassed that level. No job is too little or too large or beyond one's level or dignity, especially when it's an emergency. However, when you work remotely, you are dependent on others as you do not meet colleagues and subordinates every day. Hence, reviewing their roles on a weekly or monthly basis becomes essential as it helps improve productivity and leads to contribution from the team. It is not just you who should multitask but ensure that your teams are trained to multitask. Multitasking reduces stress and anxiety, creates backups during times of absenteeism, brings in new ideas and eventually improves productivity. It also helps on reducing costs for the company and helps employees in personal and career development.

If you work from home, you may also need to attend to virtual meetings or calls way beyond work hours, you may have to burn midnight oil to research or prepare important reports, you may have to cancel your dinner plans because something urgent came up; hence, patience, adaptability and flexibility are important traits that come along which one should be prepared for.

2. Upgrade your technology and technical skills.

Technology can work wonders and the faster you adapt, the more time and effort is saved. As Meghan worked from home, she ensured that the Wi-Fi worked excellently and that she had all types of apps that made work easy. She personally updated programmes and software using advice from her information technology head and made sure she had the best firewall system to protect data. She always researched software that would help her work remotely, especially capture and analyse reports. She upgraded her Microsoft Office skills at all times as new upgraded versions had better features that made life easier and exciting. Although she wasn't involved in handling software, she was responsible for data analysis and reports and thus was always active in tracing down software and tools, comparing them with the existing ones. She took short-term courses and shamelessly sought help from friends and even her juniors to upgrade her skills. Many of them taught her how to read reports and even reply to them. This made Meghan extremely confident as now everything was available at the click of a button. Life was literally at her fingertips and she would have it no other way.

3. Have credibility.

This is the most important trait one should possess while working remotely. Credibility means honesty and trustworthiness. Credible people do not abuse freedom and authority. It means that one would never use excuses of bad internet or network to avoid a meeting or get out of it early. One should never drop calls, stating that they ran out of battery. One should not avoid calls, bluffing that they were on another line and missed calling back. Credible people work as per requisite timelines no matter where they are and deliver high-quality results. Credible people need no supervision and do not need to be chased. They are both responsible and accountable for their jobs. It would make no difference if people with high credibility worked from office, home, another country or the moon. Today's technology supports remote working and if one wants remote working to be a way of life, then credibility has to be at its optimum. Credible people don't have to lie about not being able to complete tasks. They just need to be honest and ask for extension of timelines with justifiable reasons.

4. Make yourself available.

Making oneself available means answering the phone at all times. It means being there when people need you. Yes, you may choose to set those time limits with your teams, but do ensure that you answer your phone during work hours. Remember, we are all human beings and may need someone to talk to, share our personal lives or our troubles. Hence, if you receive calls beyond 9 p.m., it could be a colleague trying to reach you because of any of these reasons. However, you may want to draw the line on the type of calls you entertain. In case you have missed a call, ensure that you respond to it within ten to fifteen minutes. Let your team be assured that no matter how far apart you may physically be, you care as much and are empathetic. Be prepared to counsel people, give feedback during personal stress. It is not required that all direct messages should be responded to immediately. Also, it is best to talk and sort things out rather than leave them hanging or prevent them overflowing to the next day. Remember that if it is a life-and-death situation, people will call you no matter what; hence, you may choose not to revert to certain messages. Be available to your bosses in case they need something urgent from you even at wee hours. These will be one off scenarios you will be dealing with; hence, accept them if you choose to work remotely. Also, be prepared to travel without notice as there may be a situation that needs your physical presence. Know your team well and know their pulse. Be there for them as often as you can. However, do mark aside your personal and professional boundaries.

5. Have the ability to take and give frequent feedback.

Don't wait for an annual appraisal or midterm review. Take feedback about your style of management and work methodology. Don't forget to take feedback on your leadership style and people management skills. Good leaders lead from behind, provide opportunities, council during failures and encourage people to move forward. They motivate you to achieve targets, share your success stories with others and reward you through their generous emails and thank-you speeches. If you are experiencing all this, rest assured that it is an indicator that you are on the line of success.

Feedback may not always be good; hence, be prepared to handle criticism and new ways of doing things or change your working style. Remember, you are not the best at everything you do and everyone may not have that 'Midas touch'. However, being a good listener and having the desire to adapt and improve can bring you loads of success.

At the same time, share feedback with your team. Review personal performance as well as team performance and give immediate feedback. Always find out the 'whys' before you take stringent action against someone. Stand up for your team and be there during difficult times, even though you may be miles apart. Get on video chats, share personal time and ensure that they share personal joys with you. Try to build a healthy team through constant feedback both ways.

6. Have a presence on social media.

In this modern day and age where networking is crucial, having a presence on social media is highly recommended. However, it depends how active or robust you would like your social media life to be. For those who are hooked on or love this form of networking, good for you, but for those who like a slightly more private type of life, choosing your social media presence and channels becomes crucial. You may want to go for a private account or choose to be present only on professional networking sites, but all in all, ensure that you have a presence.

The right amount of networking can help you learn, participate and even venture into interests that you did not possess before. At the same time, it is important to know the opinions of world leaders, business tycoons and research firms. Social media should not be used for becoming judgemental or drawing opinions about people's lives. Hypocrisy is not the reason why you choose to be there. Engage in worthwhile conversations, take opinion polls, contribute and absorb learnings from this medium. It helps you stay connected and helps people stay connected with you. Who knows which side of the table the future may put you at?

7. Compassionate spouse and family.

Remote working is a high-pressure job which sometimes ends up working way beyond regular work hours or being unable to switch off. At times, one has to pack up overnight and travel. All this is only possible if you are either single with no strings attached or live with family that respects and understands your work and your ambitions. If you are married, then all this is only possible if you have an understanding spouse, someone who cares about you and your work, stands by you, supports you in your career and gives you unconditional flexibility. If you have children, then your spouse should be willing to play the role of both parents while you travel. Get your children to understand that your work is important to you but also get them to know that they are the most important and you would put them first in life no matter what the circumstances are. They are your first priority and no job or human being in the world can change that. For all this to become a reality, strike a good work-life balance or else, acceptance will always become a challenge.

We have highlighted the key factors required for successful remote working. Working from home or remotely does not mean that you spend the year locked up in your study or let work consume you in toto. Maintaining a work-life balance is equally crucial because, hey, you decided to opt for this mode so that you could have better quality of life. Let us assume that you save two hours a day on travelling and about an hour on grooming or getting ready to get to work. Treat your day like it had twenty-seven hours and see how much extra you can gain from life. Let us see how these three hours of extra time can add value to ourselves.

17

Your Day Has Twenty-Seven Hours

1. Socialise:

If you opt for work from home or remote working, you do interact less frequently with people. We all know that face-to-face communication whether personal or professional is something that is satisfying and helps us vent even our deepest secrets or sorrows. If all conversations that you indulge in life are only on video calls or voice calls, then it's time you get a 'LIFE'. Ensure that you meet your friends, family, community or those who you are personally connected to at least once in two weeks for a get-together. This could be over a birthday, anniversary, potluck or just Saturday night cocktails. You may choose going for a movie, a stand-up comedy, a pub or discotheque. Socialising inculcates certain behaviours and manners and also helps you with enhancing conversational skills. Apart from that, it improves your general knowledge. In case it doesn't do all of the above, it at least allows you to let down your hair and enjoy a good time which is solace for one's soul. I do not recommend you become a social butterfly, but hey, who knows? It might be good for you.

2. Treat yourself more often to the finer things in life.

In today's modern age, most of the working population enjoys going out on weekends. Whereas when you work from home, you don't have to wait for the weekend as you can use that extra time you have to dine out even on a weekday. If you believe that you earn well, then spend it wisely on yourself. Do not compromise while choosing a wine or eating at a high-end restaurant. Since you have a longer day, go dine at a fine restaurant that gives you great service, where you feel relaxed and allows you to stay back longer. You have extra time to shop, so go buy clothes that make you feel comfortable even if they cost more. Pamper yourself at a reputed salon, ask for the senior most stylist even if you have to wait for a few hours to get an appointment. Take a herbal or SPA treatment. Take time to choose cosmetics after careful comparison, ones that will not deteriorate your skin and hair by the age of 40. Most of us do not pay attention to all these details when we are young. By doing all this, I certainly don't mean 'showing off or succumbing to peer pressure'. Use your time to do the finer things in life. I am purely referring to the fact that if you believe that you have some extra time, treat yourself to things that are good for your body and those that do not have any long-term implications on its health and endurance.

3. Holiday more often.

In today's world, most people save up for travel or a vacation. A total of fifty million Indians travelled overseas in 2019. Domestic tourism figures show close to 2 billion visits in the same year. These statistics only prove the statement made earlier. Domestic tourism is diverse and accounts for 80 percent of tourism revenue for the country. Travelling is not only a vacation but is also experiential learning for some. For others, it is exploring or getting away, wellness, wildlife or nature tourism, religious or family get-togethers. Today even weddings are considered to be leisure tourism as families get away from the places they reside, to celebrate with a closely knit crowd amidst serene settings.

Whatever the reason you choose, do take a holiday. Since you work from home and exhaust only a minuscule proportion of your leave, use the rest to rejuvenate. People who work from home need frequent breaks and now since you have three hours extra to spare literally every single day, it simply means that you can leave for short weekend vacations on a Friday afternoon and get back on a Monday afternoon by putting in extra hours during working days. However, one should not take this arrangement for granted but should always confide in their superiors before taking such decisions.

While on holiday, make sure that your leisure time is not disturbed and that you have delegated your duties to the next capable person whom you have groomed to take the lead in your absence. It is obvious that if you are trekking or taking a dip in a swimming pool or the ocean or taking a SPA, it will not be possible to take calls. Set boundaries with your teams such that their calls are always welcome in case of business exigencies and if something is extremely urgent, they could leave you a message to which you will respond. Ensure that people respect your personal time off and make sure you do the same in return.

4. Pursue hobbies and step up those skills.

Moving back to the three extra hours that all you lucky people have in a day, I am really wondering what all of you do with it. Do you oversleep, binge on TV or use it to do all those things you absolutely love or generally do not find time for? If you haven't started doing that, it's never too late.

Your life is meaningless if you have no time to pursue hobbies. You might have hobbies like art, sports, reading, blogging and so on. You might have always wanted to learn a skill that would add value to your area of work, be it digital marketing, a new software or even a certification in financial modelling. You may have wanted to learn the guitar, play football with your kids or go riding with your friends.

Most individuals have more than one hobby, but when asked what those hobbies are, they would generally take a long mental haul before responding, reason being they haven't pursued their hobbies in ages and are unsure whether they still exist. Don't be in this boat. We have only one life and we should do all the things we love the most in this one life. Don't let your work situation defeat the very purpose of working remotely.

5. Have 'me time'

When was the last time you had some **'me time'**? What is **'me time'**? Once you have surpassed a certain growth level in life, you will be craving for this **'me time'**. This simply means time spent relaxing on one's own as opposed to working or doing things for others. It is seen as an opportunity to reduce stress or restore energy. All of us need this. Some of us are so caught up in life's rat race that this time ceases to exist.

We may like to spend this private time with our spiritual selves, in meditation or yoga, researching an area of interest, walking in the woods alone, or photography or cooking. At times, a 'me time holiday' becomes even more important than a 'family holiday'. 'Me time' helps in connecting with one's inner self and builds energy and inner well-being. It makes life meaningful.

Many people have discovered their real purpose in life because of this time. Many have changed their professions; many have changed lifestyles. This time should never be compromised. Even a half an hour of it in a day or a couple of hours during a weekend can add endless value to one's life. It is often said we come into the world alone and go back alone, therefore having done things that satisfy yourself and your soul does make life very meaningful and gives you that extra breathing space that you may need to die a happy soul.

6. Have family time.

The biggest positive of work from home is 'family time'. Most working professionals yearn for it. The more you grow professionally, unfortunately, the lesser of it you have. If you already feel this way, it's time to change things, my friend. Remember the reason you opted to work from home? It is simply because you wanted a good balance between work and family. Now that you have it, make the most of it.

Have a daily routine post-work. You may spend this time with your kids or gardening. You could even plan to take an afternoon or early evening break so that you can have lunch with your kids or help them with homework once they are home from school. Taking an hour off and then adding it to your day or working late to compensate can help work wonders, especially on the family bonding part. You can also help your spouse with routine household chores, call up your mother who lives in another city, speak to friends or even make weekend plans.

Ensure that your weekends and holidays are not spent dealing with visits to banks or electricity departments or doing unnecessary chores that you piled up and left for the weekend. Teach your spouse and children to do basic household chores, pitch in wherever possible. Keep your weekends for your family and overall rest and relaxation. Go places, eat great food, click loads of photos, go crazy on social media and create fantastic memories with the people you love because it is only these that will matter to you eventually.

7. Plan your finances well:

It is indeed very important to spend some extra time on planning your finances and re-evaluating them. Most of us get drowned into work and leave the financial planning for the weekend. We are then so fatigued by the weekend that we push it for the next week and the next and so on until something hits us hard on the head, leading to an increase in our blood pressure levels.

No financial institutions other than banks work on weekends, so leaving your finances to the weekends makes absolutely no sense. Also, all finances can be handled remotely literally at the click of a button or a phone call. Physical visits can be completely eliminated unless, of course, it's an insurance claim or a life insurance policy you are making, where you need to undergo a medical test. If you are a loyal customer of a financial institution, you may even be served at your doorstep.

Whether a traditional or high-risk investor, take time to evaluate your financial status. Always make provisions for important aspects such as a medical insurance, life insurance or some fixed traditional investments like fixed deposits. Put your eggs in different baskets, depending upon the corpus you plan on accumulating and the financial target you plan on achieving after certain number of years.

If you are a risk-averse investor, then stay that way as this will give you mental peace. Also, if you are an investor ready to take a gamble, ensure that you are strong enough to deal with the consequences and not get into depression. Do not invest in portfolios that can ruin your entire basket of savings or land you in debt. Retain a high credit rating score so that no bank rejects your loan application.

Remember, you are still working as you need the money to sustain yourself. You need that money to grow your existing business, you want certain level of comforts, you have families to look after or debts to pay, that money is important to treat your loved one who is suffering from an ailment and many such other reasons.

People who do not believe they work for all these reasons may be living in denial, but it is also true that people who build large successful empires are still involved in business because of emotional reasons. Many such individuals continue to remain part of the organisation and have become philanthropists and mentors to others. They dedicate a large portion of their earnings to communities and have left very little for their children. Their brands have grown to become pioneers in their respective industries because of their philanthropic values and all this was a result of good financial planning.

How Meghan Utilised That Extra Time

Let's get back to the main character of our story, 'Meghan'. She worked remotely and had some extra hours a day, which she put to great use in every city that she lived in.

She trained in salsa at the age of 32, not with her husband being her dance partner but with another student in the dance academy that she went to. She dedicated forty-five minutes to exercise every single day of her life except weekends and vacations.

During her younger days, Meghan was best described as being a tomboy. She knew everything from riding to shooting, swimming, playing sports and so on. However, after her accident, she had lost confidence in riding, something that she enjoyed the most. With some of the extra time Meghan had on her hands, she started taking the initiative to ride again. It isn't something she had forgotten. She was horribly terrified of falling off a bike again, but she also believed that she had to toughen up to do the thing she most loved. Meghan would combine a few compensatory offs to visit her mother in her hometown at least thrice a year. She could never part from her family and the wonderful people she was born and brought up with. While she was on one such trip, Meghan gathered the courage to ride again. It was cake walk for her, even though she did it after twelve years. She kept wondering how fear had dominated her from trying all these years. This was a moment of self-realisation. She learnt that one must have the heart to take the plunge in case one truly wants to achieve something and that it doesn't mean that one should stop trying if one has fallen no matter how hard it hurt.

Meghan always believed in moving ahead with times. She had become active on social media and even took a professional course in digital marketing. As a student, Meghan had won many accolades for her oratory and presentation skills. It was tough then as there were no tools to help one better their speech or content, but this shortcoming has taken a turnaround in today's digital world. Being inspired by travel writers and journalists, Meghan began her own blog and also started contributing to magazines and journals. This was another eye opener where Meghan learnt that a balanced life could help you pursue your passions. Writing was not a hobby for Meghan, it was pure passion. To Meghan, it was as good as yoga. It was an art where she could pour out her heart and mind and bring out the best in her. Not just that, the writings could also be shared on multiple platforms for others to read and benefit.

Meghan also learnt to trade in shares. She would study stocks and take advice from her friends in the financial sectors on the best buys. She did make some handsome returns by the side and still invests and monitors the performance of existing stocks.

On the home front, Meghan spent a lot of time collecting paintings, curios and other artefacts. She was an admirer of glassware and linen. Thanks to the internet and the spare time she took from vacations, she would spend time decorating and redecorating the house. She spent a lot of time with plants and growing her own kitchen garden.

Working remotely also gave Meghan the time to pursue her passion for photography. She had a natural knack for it, but a professional camera that Anand had purchased for himself became part of Meghan's travel kit as Anand never really got the time for his hobbies. Meghan had spent time experimenting and taking lessons on YouTube. Apart from using the camera for food and travel photography, which she absolutely loved, she used it in her profession as well. Some of those stunning pictures are even on the company website and renowned magazines and yes, one may never know of this as Meghan never craved for photo credits. She volunteered to do it, simply because she loved it.

Meghan and Stephanie were more like sisters. Meghan spent her spare time chatting about her childhood days and all the fun she had outdoors which today's kids unfortunately don't. She spent adequate time enhancing Stephanie's tennis, cycling and swimming skills. They would both listen to music and even have their own karaoke parties. Meghan also took Stephanie to yoga classes and personally coached her in maths. They would set out together on long drives and even vacation all by themselves...... just the two of them. Anand had a job that consumed his entire life and Meghan knew that the best way to maintain the balance and play the role of both parents was to have a well-balanced job. The money, position and office appreciation was secondary to her. It was a choice she had willingly made and was ready to accept its downsides.

She always focussed on the upsides of what she had, rather than the flipside of what was missing. A truly happy soul, Meghan was the envy of many people, both professionally and personally.

Time passed and the company was happy with Meghan's performance. They knew that she could take up larger responsibilities. Meghan knew people, processes and the hotel business like the back of her hands. She had also been involved in many community programmes.

Over the last four to five years, the trend of sabbaticals has made headways to more women joining the workforce, leading to a better female-to-male ratio. However, ten years ago, the scenario was very different. Women would generally drop out of work during pregnancy or post-pregnancy as they needed to devote time towards child care. They also got only three months of maternity leave and at times, were forced out of the job as organisations could not hold on to their positions beyond three months without taking a replacement. Then when they tried to get back to work, there was a so-called questionable gap in their résumés, which led to unfavourable recruitment. This would mean accepting either a lower position or a compromised salary.

However, Meghan did not have to go through all this as she had moved from an advisory to a full-time portfolio with the same company that she was consulting for. She knew the core team and believed in the ethics and culture of the new company. She had conveyed her inability to report to work daily and was offered remote working with a very high-pressure job and targets that were difficult to achieve. She accepted to travel wherever and whenever the company wanted her to. Meghan often left her 6-year-old at home and travelled for days at a stretch. Her phone and laptop were her office and she made everything possible. She filled in the void between her family and herself through video calls and keeping Sundays completely free for the family. Her superiors were kind enough and very encouraging. They offered her privacy and treated her like family. All this only motivated Meghan to believe that she had taken a step in the right direction. However, the most trying part when you don't report to office every day is relationship management with teams.

18

Making long distance relationships successful

A lot of couples separate or get divorced in real life as they cannot maintain long-distance relationships. Working with a team remotely also has similar challenges, the main one being **'trust'** and the next being **'misunderstanding'**. Forbearance, trust, sacrifice, support, humility, zero egos, good listening skills are all important traits of a healthy and successful relationship.

Let's take a look at what one should do to keep it together.

1. Talk to people frequently.

The success of any relationship can be gauged by what and how you communicate. Communication can be effective only when the recipient has received a message in the manner it was meant to be interpreted. You would have often played the game 'Chinese whispers' or 'broken telephone'. In this game, there is a chain of players where the first player whispers a sentence into the second player's ears and by the time the message reaches the last player, the message is completely distorted. This does happen very often in our lives and with the advent of messaging especially WhatsApp, it is even more frequent. Written and verbal communication are two different forms and should be used for the right kind of messages.

Very often, WhatsApp messages start out productively and end up disastrously. This is because somewhere there is a misunderstanding. Very often, a message that was proposed to be sent to an individual reaches another just because one pressed the wrong button. While these mediums have their own advantages, it is very important to verbally communicate with people. Pick up the phone or get on to a video call and communicate to your team. Have a video meeting at least once in a week. Make a connection that goes way beyond voice and one that can be replaced with a face.

There is a very famous saying, 'It's always easier when you have a face to the voice'. The very fact that you want to see people no matter how far they are makes your team believe that you genuinely care about them and look forward to seeing them. Apart from follow-ups and their schedules, make time for some informal discussions and seek their opinions in decision-making. Let the communication always flow both ways.

Arguments and discussions can achieve great results if they are kept healthy.

2. Stop thinking what. Think how much.

Most often, superiors wonder what subordinates do, either at their seats in the office, on sales calls or while working from home. The mind is the creator of all evil. Don't let your blood pressure rise by thinking about what people do. Just focus on productivity. If you have productivity, which means quality and quantity within stipulated time lines, you and your team will accomplish your goals. You could have a flexible agreement with everyone in your team, but you must ensure that people understand the importance of goals and the methods of achieving them. To achieve productivity, you must set the processes in place right from the start. Have reporting systems, structures and schedules that help both you and your team connect with ease and efficiency. Monitor performance and give regular feedback. Help individuals raise their productivity through your management skills in a way that you never have to worry about how they are spending their time. The only thing you should focus upon is your confidence levels in that individual. If people have achieved their targets and have time to spare, give it to them on a platter. Send them home early, throw in a surprise for them, give them a day off. They will value you even more and give you better than their best. If you are not doing this, then it's time to change as no matter how hard you try, your relationship will never work out if you are not obliging and encouraging.

3. Know people both professionally and personally.

At times, we have teams with diverse individuals. Some may have spent years within the company and some may have joined the team recently. Well, in both cases, one must understand each human being in the team, their strengths and weaknesses, family backgrounds, cultures, aspirations, even remember their birthdays and also understand if there are any stressors or downturns that team members are currently experiencing. Sometimes even the best performer may not be able to deliver high productivity and that may not be because they have gotten lazy or are shunning work. Such situations can be the outcome of personal problems, fatigue or health issues.

You may not be able to help at all times, but if you know people well, you can work out enduring relationships. The moment your team feels 'care and concern', you will begin to experience their loyalty. Every relationship has a little bit of 'give and take', so don't only keep taking, also learn to give. Give them space and an opportunity to get up if they fall. Lend a patient ear to their problems. Know their families, their hobbies and their aspirations. Pitch in to help wherever you can. Let your team know that you are there for them and in return, they will be there when you need them the most even if they have to burn the midnight oil.

Your professional relationship is only at work and you can be as good as family or a friend outside the work periphery. However, don't let friendship or your relationship with people get tiring or stressful when it comes to reprimanding. There should be a marked difference between your professional relationship and personal relationship. You may be a great guide, counsellor or even a mentor, but don't let these positive traits overpower performance standards. Many employees draw close relationships with their superiors just to have them on their right sides. These are self-centred relationships and a good superior should realise the difference between the two. In no circumstances should there be a compromise on performance or over quality of work, no matter how close you are to your team.

4. Stop remote supervision.

Remote supervision is a very common factor that ruins relationships. Often, bosses text their subordinates at odd hours, not allowing them to switch off. Others keep tabs on their lunch breaks, how many times they left their desk, the time they clocked in and out, etc. All these factors depict lack of trust and can ruin a relationship. Bosses are often nicknamed as Hitlers, policemen, commanders, not to forget names of some of our popular Bollywood villains like 'Gabbar'. I'm certain no boss enjoys such nicknames. Trust cannot be built overnight and has to be cultivated over time. This may take three to six months, but do it patiently and wholeheartedly. It will go a long way and way beyond establishing merely a professional relationship.

5. Walk the talk.

Surprise people with your creativity and innovation. Discuss a new development that they can all be part of. Send greeting cards or flowers on their birthdays. When you decide to visit the office, make sure that you have lunch with your team and even take them out for a drink. If you have travelled on a holiday, get them a small memento or even a chocolate made in that region. If you can afford to pick up the tab, buy them a great wine from your overseas trip. It is very important to know the tastes, likes and dislikes of your team. When they go on holidays, encourage them to send photographs. Click team photos, encourage them to participate in team activities, corporate social responsibility initiatives, competitions and external volunteering programmes. Share the stage with them when you win awards. Train them to prioritise tasks, handle difficult situations, leave their desks or log off in time. Give them credit for their achievements. When you visit the office, walk the floors with them, have lunch in the cafeteria with the team or just hang around in the lobby area or the lawns to engage in informal conversations. If you live in the same city, invite them home. Insist on visiting their homes at times even if you don't mean to. Recommend a known doctor or a travel agent on your own, even if they have not requested for one. This will make them admire your leadership skills and believe that you are completely into them. One important thing here, don't just follow the above points on paper. GET OUT THERE AND MAKE IT HAPPEN.

6. Recruit people who possess integrity.

Now this is a tricky one and often difficult to evaluate, but hey, not impossible. Senior leaders should be involved in any management level recruitment as they have tons of experience in dealing with all kinds of people, that their 'gut feel' is seriously contributory to the success of the recruitment process. Have a three-way interview process (peer, immediate superior and boss). Stretch the interview meeting in at least three parts rather than having just one. For long-distance interviews, choose a face time meeting even if the person is being recruited for a technical or back-of-the-house job. Wherever face-to-face meetings are possible, have them in the offices or have them socially. Behavioural changes are always better gauged in social settings rather than formal office interviews.

Apart from evaluating factors like past experiences, achievements and personal hobbies or traits, focus on value- and ethics-based questions. Find out whether the person is involved in any personal volunteering programmes, is part of any club or society/trust or association, the kind of accolades the person has achieved in the past, their views and opinions on political leaders, current affairs, any favourite sports hero or movie star, journalist, philanthropist and so on. In addition to all this, understand the family background and family values of individuals, the hardships they have faced or whether they were born with a golden spoon. All these are factors that help you gauge the attitude and value traits of the candidate.

This will also help you assess whether the person's values match yours and whether the person would be a cultural fit for your organisation. You may have a person with great experience, but it is only high-integrity levels that can determine infusion into your culture. Do background checks not just with previous organisations the person has worked in but also ex-colleagues. If the individual has three or less years of work experience, cross-check with the educational institution from where the candidate has graduated. Get an evaluation of the character, traits and performance of the individual. Don't ever judge a book by its cover. Ensure that you read all its pages before you critique it.

Recruitment may be a cumbersome process and when a candidate applies to your organisation, you must communicate the stages and period that this recruitment exercise may get extended to. Let candidates be prepared and not form any negative impression about your organisation. Communicate periodically about the next round and once the process has been completed, communicate the decision to the candidate. This will avoid unnecessary phone calling by the candidate to understand the status of her/his candidature.

All this seems like a tedious process for human resource professionals and head hunters, but why not? You intend to spend at least the next two years with the individual, if not more, so wouldn't you want to have the right hire? In addition, you will have a long-distance relationship with the candidate. Else, you end up firing someone within three to six months of joining. Fifty percent of attrition in an organisation occurs because we do not hire the right individuals, because we only judge candidates based upon their work experience. Another 50 percent of attrition occurs because of bad bosses. Hence, whatever level you are recruiting at, don't mess it up. Make an investment of your personal time that will add to the top-line productivity in the long run.

Once an employee feels totally connected with you, trust will never be a deterring factor. However, not all outcomes can be positive and you may find people not being able to cope up with work from home or remote working. This you will be able to gauge by evaluating the productivity of the person. While setting your key performance indicators and subsequently key result areas, 90 percent of your goals should be made measurable and a 10 percent buffer can always be dedicated towards core values, ethics and other soft traits. This could also be an 80–20 ratio, depending upon the job profile or role, but ensure that your goals follow the SMART approach (specific, measurable, achievable, realistic and time-bound).

Goal Setting Depends upon a Variety of Factors, Including

1. Company's past performance
2. Innovation or new product launch
3. Prevailing market conditions
4. Government regulations
5. Sales and marketing efforts
6. Availability of resources
7. Partnership performances
8. Internal efforts

A good manager must remember if his team fails, so does she/he. Also, although a formal performance appraisal is conducted once a year, goals need to be reviewed and at times altered to remain on track. This could mean creating new ways of achieving targets, reviewing the profit and loss account more frequently, watching expenses, motivating people, encouraging innovation, conducting frequent reviews of sales and marketing efforts and so on. Involvement of all individuals and resources should be considered during reviews to make goals achievable.

19

Meghan Takes up Multiple Challenges

Three years into the system and Meghan's learning was getting even more exciting. She was moved into a sales and marketing function, which was not new to her as she had an academic qualification and loads of creativity to back up this new role. In addition, she had completed digital marketing courses with the extra time she got working from home.

Those working in sales and marketing functions of large organisations will agree that this function can consume your life. It is not time-bound and one of little appreciation. Also, selling is not always easy, especially for a product that is new or has a small market. Meghan knew what she was getting into. She worked relentlessly day and night to formulate new strategies by self-educating herself and taking help from her friends and colleagues in the industry. Today's new era of marketing has moved from print to digital and technology has advanced to an extent that it is changing rapidly.

Coping with this development itself is a huge challenge for all marketers. The function is one of precision and cannot afford mistakes, especially if it involves any kind of media publicity. I am certain all marketers out there will agree to how meticulous and time-consuming their jobs are. They have to strive for perfection, anticipate customer needs, come up with new marketing strategies all the time, build excellent relationships with customers and be extremely careful about their language and tone of voice in all forms of communication.

Those heading senior positions in this function also realise all the risks associated with the job, but this did not stop Meghan. She looked at it as a different challenge and took it up with 100 percent dedication. During the course of this function, she met up with many journalists and writers. There were many 'eureka moments' in her life. There were some people who had given up everything to pursue their love for travelling. Many had become famous bloggers and writers, others had merely stepped into this profession a few years ago but had already received their calling. They passionately narrated their work to her and at times, Meghan felt that she was almost a part of their story. This was yet another 'moment of truth' for Meghan. This was the moment where she was now convinced that life was way beyond earning good money. It was about being happy with whatever you do. You can be happy irrespective of who you are. You can be a pioneer in a niche market, a hero at your home or a role model to your colleagues and friends. Some of us make it to stardom and some are stars in the eyes of their loved ones for the simplest of things they manage to achieve.

All these writers had no offices, they worked from home. Even those who worked for large publishing houses worked and travelled out of home. Meghan would often read their blogs and social media posts which showcased their writing desks, balconies and other spots in the house where their creative abilities triggered incredibly. She got to know of many writers who quit their jobs, saved up money to travel up to the mountains or even abroad to pursue their passion for writing. This is just one cadre of people we are talking about in the marketing function, but as time progressed, Meghan came across dozens of people who serviced large corporations through digital platforms and virtual interactions all carried out of home. It's funny how superiors would question subordinates if they chose to Work From Home for a day due to personal reasons, but how receptive and accommodating they are when a job function is outsourced. We do not care if the individual we are collaborating with works from the moon. All we care about is the results being qualitative and time-bound. Not that we were doing this for a lesser price with no guarantee of the content being kept confidential. Who knows whether the individual also services our competition? Yet we treat them with dignity and respect and allow them leverage even if tasks are not completed. Imagine if we did this for our own employees, I am certain they would take a bullet for us.

Meghan always played by company policies but still went out of her way to help her teams both professionally and personally. She was always available over the phone and travelled to the hotel sites once a quarter and to the headquarters at least twice a month. She had never refused to show up for an unplanned meeting even if it meant travelling to another state unless, of course, she was unwell or had certain prior obligations which she could not break. Flexibility was her second name and humility was third. She always got along with all sorts of people, be it personally or professionally and that included even the office boy and driver. She had goodies and stories for everyone. She ensured that she took on the role with passion and commitment.

Meghan further progressed into an analyst's role which she thoroughly enjoyed, teasing the grey matter in her brains. She would analyse profit and loss accounts and come up with methods to make financial progress. Although not directly involved in cost-cutting as she was not handling an operations portfolio, Meghan made sure that her checks and balances were in place. She worked with the sales teams on effective methods of tapping new market segments to increase revenue. She worked on marketing techniques that would increase brand visibility. She was clued on to 'customer satisfaction' as she strongly believed that customer satisfaction led to business growth. Earning a brand reputation isn't easy with the competition that surrounds you and if one holds themselves up high on a horse just because they are working with a predominantly good brand, then they are fooling themselves. Brand loyalty can be gained only through customer satisfaction and in today's world, **'satisfaction'** isn't just enough, customers must be **'DELIGHTED'**.

As Meghan grew within the company, she moved on to a strategic role, which simply meant working on increasing the company's profitability and branding, battling its competitors. This meant dealing with management information systems, sales and marketing, human resources and corporate social responsibility. All these roles consumed Meghan's day, but thanks to the remote working agreement, Meghan was able to cope up with it all. While her husband left for work at 9 a.m. and returned only post 9 p.m., Stephanie would leave for school at 6.30 a.m. and return at 3.30 p.m. Meghan was an early morning person and started at her day at the study at 8:30 a.m. She would complete seven hours of work by 3:30 p.m., right in time to receive Stephanie at home.

Meghan had no household chores to do. That is the way she had planned her life. The cooking, cleaning, laundry and other chores were all outsourced. There were absolutely no distractions. Meghan cleaned her study herself and did not let anyone enter it. She would also dedicate three hours a week post 7 p.m. to help Stephanie cope up with her homework. After a short afternoon break at the dining table with Stephanie, Meghan would return back to work and try to close her day by 7 p.m. However, the lights of her study were on till 9 p.m. and she would send any report or take calls until then. Meghan had set her cut-off time to be 9 p.m. She was one of those women who lived up to meeting deadlines and proactively requested for extensions in case of delays. Being reminded was something she disliked.

Meghan followed a traditional diary system as a scheduler. She carried forward tasks that she wasn't able to complete only if they were not on her priority list. If they were priorities, she made sure that she would not shut shop until those were completed.

Meghan moved many states but always ensured that the house she rented would have a built-in study or an additional room that she could convert into a study. She never worked out of her bedroom as she believed that it did not make her feel like a professional. She strongly believed that one should not have too many electronic devices in the bedroom as it leads to anxiety and disruption of sleep patterns, which is extremely harmful to one's health. Meghan felt that she was able to strike a good balance between work and home. However, she never mixed the two and there was not a day in her life that she was reminded of not doing a good job by her superiors because she worked from home. This was not only because Meghan had proven herself valuable but also because her promoters were futuristic leaders and put quality, trust and timelines above all. Meghan valued her CEO's leadership style. A humble, charismatic and compassionate leader, he empowered his teams without stepping on their toes. Not a day in her life did she feel insecure or less worthy of herself. All she cared about was giving her best. What mattered more to her were simple gestures of appreciation like being invited over to her CEO's house for a family dinner, an office lunch whenever she went to work, a simple conversation on the industry or even a one-line message saying 'Thank you' or 'Well done'.

20

Life After Work – Discussing Joys, Shedding Guilt and Building Dreams

I would again like to reiterate that Meghan's aspirations were different and very unlike others in the corporate world. Generally, evenings at home are for discussions with spouse on how each one spent their day, how people screwed up and all the other insecurities that get people gossiping. Meghan always had work on her mind and, at times, would be drowned with phone calls from colleagues, but she wasn't into badmouthing people. In fact, time after work was to tell Anand stories about all the people she helped – the handicapped girl who is tremendously talented, the widow who has two children to feed and cannot afford to lose her job, the charity that she desperately wants to raise funds for but can't find the time and so on. Her discussions were all about improving the quality of life for others.

The rest of the discussions were on their retirement plans, furnishing of their house, refurbishment of a classic car nearing vintage that they owned and an RV that she always wanted to build. Both Meghan and Anand chose to spend their evenings together chatting about their dreams and the good things in life. They often played cards, flipped through old photographs and watched movies together every weekend. How grateful they were for having each other and Stephanie. There were many times Meghan cried with guilt of not being able to spend enough time with Stephanie and, at times, missing her school annual day because she was travelling. There were times when Stephanie was unwell and Meghan was unable to attend to her because she was on work in another city. Meghan had to take many calculated calls and striking that balance was not always easy. She would often feel depressed but then hold up and decide to make it up to Stephanie in ways that she enjoyed the most. On the positive side, Stephanie had become very independent. She developed qualities like patience, problem solving and good listening skills at a very early age. She was truly disciplined and gave Meghan enough personal space. She very well knew how much Meghan's job meant to her and always supported her by organising her phone book or helping her with Social Media Marketing.

Meghan received incessant support from Anand. He too had made many sacrifices so that the two of them could stay together. Meghan was very clear about one thing and that is if the choice had to ever be made between living apart or staying together, she would give up her job and choose family. Both her mother and her mother-in-law always came to her rescue when she had to travel for longer periods or when both she and Anand had to travel for work at the same time. One thing in life she never did was leave Stephanie with the maids. She cared too much about her safety and wellbeing. By the tone of her voice during this interview, I knew that no job in the world could woo her into compromising on Stephanie's safety.

21

The Path towards Self-Actualisation

As time progressed within the organisation, Meghan was pleasantly surprised one morning when introduced to a formal philanthropic role, one that she accepted without a blink of an eye. Her CEO had observed her passion for the community and felt that she would be a great fit for leading its philanthropic mission. Meghan was truly grateful as she now believed that she was stepping on the path of self-actualisation. She had some good organisations that she had worked for in the past, including a start-up at the age of 27 and now was introduced to a senior corporate role that was not just another job but also a passion.

Meghan travelled the country to set up community projects. She walked muddy fields, visited women in slums and hutments, carried under nourished infants in her arms and worked with the specially-abled. This is the second time she was witnessing poverty and disease up close, so close that she was realising how lucky she was just to have a set of hands, limbs and eyes.

There were so many people she came across who had nothing to offer except their blessings for helping them out and this was indeed the biggest gift that Meghan savours from the role. She was doubly convinced that this is what she wanted to continue doing both professionally and personally as she felt successful even when she clothed children or provided them with a basic education.

Most of us relate success to large achievements and accolades, but Meghan tried to make every little project she worked on successful. Working from home gave Meghan time to connect with young students, teachers and even mothers from marginalised communities over the phone. All the time that she would have spent travelling to office just to prove that she was working was the time that she used for meticulous thinking, planning and connecting with people. It is truly a blessing today that even rural India has good network connectivity and video calls are possible. Professionally every project cannot be executed or funded, but yes, it can be personally supported in many ways which Meghan did not hesitate to do. She threaded life's path with enthusiasm and great passion and did not believe that any role for her is too trivial. She measured personal success through happiness, emotional and spiritual quotients and organisational success through the appreciation from various stakeholders.

Remote working had worked out wonderfully for Meghan even pre–COVID-19. However, everyone is not Meghan and every role is not the same. Having said that, there are definitely at least 25 percent roles in every organisation that can be performed remotely. Today many information technology firms claim that they can carry out 75 percent of their work remotely. COVID-19 has been an eye-opener and they are investing in technology to make this happen efficiently. It is a proven fact that roles like sales and marketing, consulting, customer relationship management, strategy, legal, stockbroking and corporate social responsibility can be comfortably carried out remotely as these involve more contact with external stakeholders than internal ones. However, when the COVID-19 pandemic hit us, organisations realised that remote working could move way beyond the functions we have discussed here. They are also conducive to the financial sector, software support, administration, payroll, teaching, digital marketing and many other functions that have lesser human intervention and are more technologically driven. These need to be supported by a strong human resource policy framework.

Let us take a look at the advantages an organisation can gain through remote working policies.

22

Advantages to organisations that follow remote working

1. Reduced infrastructure and operational costs

By facilitating work from home, organisations will be saving on millions of dollars. Their variable costs will drop considerably, be it electricity, water, internet, cafeteria, toiletries, printing, paper or even housekeeping costs. Expenses on fixed assets such as furniture and office equipment will reduce, so will repair and maintenance. Companies can also adopt a policy wherein they fund only 20 percent of the office equipment, be it a laptop, phone or printer and the employee pays 80 percent as the property is always at the mercy of the employee. The policy can be rolled for a three-year period, considering that the life of such equipment is not longer. Such policies reduce cost on expensive office equipment and also, at the same time, give employees a choice of the brand, model and colour of the electronic equipment that they desire to work with. Companies in larger metro cities will no longer have to rent out phenomenally large office spaces to accommodate people. They would hire them from within the city or cities with good connectivity and would require people to travel for important internal or client meetings, training and development programmes, etc. It is not only the office rentals that will drop but also costs associated with parking rentals and fees will reduce considerably. This will reduce the overall operational costs of a company.

2. Reduced compensation cost

Although compensation costs do form a part of overall employee cost to company, here we are referring to costs directly related to salary. Organisations can develop different compensation strategies based upon the job profile, experience and deliverables. One can move to Gig workers or hiring experts as retainers in order to reduce the burden on statutory compliances, leave encashment, gratuity and other mandatory obligations. Others can hire people for specific projects through temping services, fixed-term contracts or outsourcing companies. Most of all, what millennials want is flexibility with a fair pay. A lot of women want to return back from sabbaticals and are looking for flexibility at work. Our country has a lot of physically challenged people who cannot travel as the public transport system in India is not travel-friendly. Tap these potential employees and create space in your organisation for them. Depending upon their role and your employment agreement with them, you could pay them a fair market price, an above-market price or even a below-market price. Flexible working arrangements can lead to flexible compensation structures that are a lower financial burden to organisations as people joining your organisation are already aware of what they are getting into and would be joining you for your flexible structure and good cultural practices.

3. Reduced travel cost

Today with most meetings being conducted virtually, executives don't need to catch a flight or stay in expensive hotels to facilitate travel. Although technology was available even before the pandemic, there was always a mental apprehension about virtual meetings and it would take days for two parties to arrive at a mutually agreeable date and time to have a face to face meeting. Not to forget decisions like which city, which hotel and whether it would be over breakfast or lunch. Some last-minute meetings cost a bomb on travel and hotel expenses. Technology can facilitate virtual meetings across the globe and thus save a company millions. It also helps in having multiple meetings on the same day, thus saving loads of time and helps execute quicker decision-making. What's even more advantageous is that all timelines are met with little or no excuses of one being unavailable.

4. Hiring the best talent pool

Flexible work environments can bring in the best talent pool from across the country and globally. With the use of technology and airports sprouting out in all cities large or small, organisations have access to people all the time. At times, one can fly into a city faster than the time taken to drive within the same city because of traffic conditions. Companies that have a national or global presence will benefit largely from a remote working structure. They will be able to understand and deliver customer requirements with ease. More diversity will lead to better performance and eventually, global brand recognition. Employees themselves will become brand ambassadors and will commit to their responsibilities with passion and dedication.

5. Contributing towards the environment

A country like India faces a huge pollution crisis, which becomes visible to the naked eye during winters. India stands amongst the top 10 polluted countries in the world with its capital city being the most polluted, followed by other metro cities and smaller towns in certain states. Since India is not supported by a good public transportation network and carpooling is almost non-existent, most individuals end up taking their own vehicles to work. This causes traffic issues, accidents and heightened level of carbon emissions, which further cause respiratory disorders in individuals.

Secondly, India still has a strong taxi network in many cities with cars that operate with Euro 2 engines as not all cities enforce scrapping of cars after a period of fifteen years. Organisations that are seriously environment-conscious should consider remote working or easing daily reporting structures to a five-day week or even a three-day week wherever possible. A classic example is how we have unknowingly contributed to bringing down the Air Quality Index value to 90 from the previous levels of above 350 by staying home during the lockdown. If organisations take the onus to categorise jobs that require daily reporting and those that don't, they will automatically reduce the burden on Mother Earth and humanity by reducing the carbon footprint.

6. Lesser absenteeism

In most circumstances, employees mainly call in sick or take leave of absence because they need to attend to a family member that is unwell. In very few circumstances, it is observed that the employee is unwell themselves. Many people apply for leave as they have to take their kids for immunisation, attend an annual function, have a doctor's appointment and so on. They are forced to apply for leave as they can't simply leave their workplaces or report to work a few hours late. This absence at work may cause many inconvenient situations for employers and at times, may lead to customer complaints or delay in implementation of important projects.

However, adopting a flexible working pattern will help employees attend to their personal issues and stretch their flexibility in completing tasks that were assigned to them. Given the opportunity of flexible or remote working, they will ensure that they balance both their professional and personal lives. It may so happen that one needs two to three weeks of leave to heal a broken bone or provide medical care to a family member suffering from an ailment. In this case, an employee may be completely capable of performing all job-related functions, but since there is no such policy made available by the company, the employee is forced to take leave and stay home. In such cases, not only has the employee to deal with backlog when they report back, but the organisation too suffers as long pending files may lead to many complications.

7. Higher retention

It is often known and accepted that favours are an outcome of something good that one had done for the other. Flexibility may not be outlined in the same fashion but is closely related. As human beings, we are always grateful when someone helps us out and we are ready to pay off this gratitude in many forms. Employees who choose flexible working are generally more dedicated than regular employees. They have chosen to work in an organisation with remote working policies, else, they could have been in any office for nine hours a day. This simply means that their comfort or necessity has led them to choose an employer who has remote working policies. They value their appointment more than others and are willing to go that extra mile to get things done. Such employees generally have high credibility and are willing to accept responsibility even if things go wrong rather than blame it on circumstances. This builds more confidence between employer and employee, builds credible relationships and increases employee retention.

8. Goodwill

Very often as organisations, we are challenged by our people and our processes. Closer to the employee satisfaction survey, we end up organising employee get-togethers, making them coffee at the office or suddenly getting involved in understanding their personal lives. Well, people are not fools to fall prey to such bribes. Overnight affection can never be real. Goodwill has to be earned and cannot be developed overnight. Secondly, it cannot be gained even after months of training or even after a promotion. An organisation can build goodwill through multiple methods, flexibility being one of them. Employees who have flexible working arrangements end up appreciating and recommending the organisation to others. They automatically start sharing their satisfaction and contentment with others. They are not ill-spoken and do not spread rumours. They share good practices on social media platforms and are more involved in engagement initiatives. All this eventually leads to better satisfaction scores and apart from paper surveys, we all acknowledge that word of mouth is the best publicity which is automatically captured as a result of good employment practices.

9. Employee health and well-being

When employees travel less frequently to office, they remain lesser exposed to threats arising out of viral infections, diarrhoea and pollution. Eating home cooked meals, avoiding use of public toilets or common cutlery and crockery can all lead to well-being of the gut and eventually, well-being of the employee. Similarly, lesser exposure to outdoors or surfaces leads to lesser chances of contracting viral infections and respiratory disorders. You will be amazed to know that most diarrhoea and stomach infection cases are due to certain common touchpoints that may be unavoidable. All these factors have a direct impact on employees' health. Employees who are healthy have better immunity and are both mentally and physically stronger. They less often fall ill and are able to cope up with hefty travel as well as long working hours. They automatically develop superior immunity levels. This results in reduced medical expenses for both the employer and employee, including reduced absenteeism.

If we consolidate all our experiences both from the employee and organisational perspective, rest assured you will realise that you did not have to get to office every single day of the week. There were many things that could have been completed from home. All we have to do as organisations is challenge those roles that can be handled remotely and those that need office reporting. Once we are able to draw that distinction and have processes to support these functions, we will realise that creating flexible environments has a positive impact both on the organisation and its employees.

23

Methods to develop remote working strategies

1. Have strong human resource policies.

This is the first step to creating a remote working environment. Human resource policies should begin by firstly categorising job roles that can be performed entirely from home, those that may need 75 percent or 50 percent presence and those that may need presence only on a case-to-case basis such as meetings and so on. Furthermore, employee benefits should be amended in terms of shift hours, leave pattern, outdoor duties and similar other factors. The human resource policies should be centred around creating a culture of trust and flexibility. At the same time, there should be no compromise around productivity.

Strong induction programmes, refresher training and self-development programmes will be the basis of creating flexible environments. Policies pertaining to leave, absenteeism and disciplinary action should be made clear at the very beginning. Goals should be defined at the beginning of every year and a structured approach to achieving these goals should be communicated to the employee. If clarity in human resource policies exists in black and white and is also made available on the human resources portal, it becomes simple for an employee to follow the same. A human resource helpdesk or a knowledge hub would be an added advantage for guidance and interpretation of policies.

2. Recruit right.

No organisation can be successful without the right set of people. Some of us may have a bunch of people that we inherit and others get opportunities to build new teams. The next step would be to identify candidate specifications for those roles. Most roles have to be high on integrity, experience and skills. If you have decided to go in for a remote working system, ensure that you offer it to only those employees who are already high on integrity. Ensure that you have done a thorough background check on credibility, integrity and teamwork like explained earlier in this book, if you decide on hiring new teams. Do not compromise these core values for any kind of experience. Also, human resources should ensure that those employees who work remotely are flexible with working hours and travel. They should have private spaces that they can work from which are disturbance-free and will not cause any impact or embarrassment during a virtual client meeting. Human resource heads must focus on developing a selection matrix for every job profile which has higher weightage for certain parameters because they are performed remotely. If this is successfully implemented, the next step would be to have an efficient remote monitoring system that could be a mix of human intervention and technology-enabled devices such as choosing to invest in certain apps that can record attendance or client meetings (virtually or in person).

3. Create future workplaces.

Future workplaces are no longer just excerpts from *Star Trek* or *Avengers*. They have certainly become a reality and are here to stay. Creating future workplaces first requires an accepting mind set from CEOs, board of directors and human resource heads. Then next is a financial investment in the form of state-of-the-art technology which is no longer unaffordable. There are many virtual meeting platforms that organisations can invest in for smooth and effective meetings. In addition to investing in a good laptop with effective storage space and speed, the ergonomic efficiency of equipment should also be considered. Organisations that have flexible work environments should create well-ventilated and clutter-free workspaces. TV rooms, coffee lounges, gaming rooms and lifestyle cafes is what the world is moving to even in office buildings. All these facilities increase motivation and create pride in the mind of an employee about the workspace. Organisations can also extend future workplaces to those employees who work from home in terms of short-term loans confined to procurement of specific office furniture and equipment that assists them in generating higher productivity. Future workplaces whether from office or home require continuous upgrade of skills and technology, hence organisations should consider these factors while creating their annual operating plans.

4. Communicate effectively.

Whether in person or remotely, communication is the key to successful relationships. Face-to-face communication is definitely more effective as it involves body language and facial expressions. However, telephonic communication or even emails at times can be wrongly interpreted and may cause a huge gap in relationship management.

While companies adapt to remote working, it is of primary importance that they consider talking more frequently rather than relying on emails, be it with their clients or their teams. Video calling at least once a week, if not more, makes one feel more acknowledged. Today's technology has features of both video and voice on virtual platforms. As a good leader, encourage and impose video calls at least once a week. A face to the voice is extremely essential in nurturing relationships.

Since you are away and not in physical contact, do not work in isolation. Take advice or suggestions if you are struggling with things or need to improve a flow chart or a presentation. Do not let your ego lure you into stopping yourself from asking a subordinate for help. If you have made a decision about a particular subject matter, ensure that the team knows about it. Keep communication short and simple.

Do not create unnecessary phone groups and expect people to stay updated through messaging. Do not assume that your teams read all messages and do not hold them accountable for that. The time that we spend on WhatsApp messages is amazingly unproductive and a complete waste of time whereas we could have picked up the phone and called. What's even worse is that it impacts our eyesight incredibly and makes the eye muscles weaker. Only effective communication can bridge misunderstandings, which would include talking to people as often as one can or writing emails to communicate important decisions or plans. Don't let messaging take over the power of verbal communication just because it is available for free or because you find it the easy way out.

Also, remember that there is communication meant just for your information and some serious communication that needs to stay on record. These should generally be done through official emails and shared with people concerned. Email etiquette can be pretty challenging at times with people not keeping the right persons in the email copy or keeping unnecessary people on the carbon copy. Keeping trail emails as a proof of continuous correspondence and organising one's inbox can prove to be extremely valuable, especially during a handover process or during an investigation or audit. It is of primary importance for all organisations to define email rules and etiquette and train people on the same.

Any organisational announcement welcoming a new business head should be communicated formally via email, but the reporting team should be informed first before that information is made public so that its confidence and trust is won. Frequent communication on new products or processes should be communicated through audio visuals and pictorial representations wherever possible to enable every employee understand the developments of the company they are working for without having to rely on other sources. Effective communication can bridge misunderstandings because people get first-hand information on that development.

Many *Fortune* 500 companies already have employee, customer and vendor satisfaction surveys implemented through software and mobile apps which again is a form of effective communication that reaches out to stakeholders, whose responses prove to be a valuable source of feedback.

Most of all communication should lead to trust building and complete understanding of the subject no matter what channel it takes. Hence, it is imperative for organisations to review their communication processes frequently.

5. Engage workforce.

Individuals that work from home may feel cut off and not aligned to the day-to-day office events. Also, since they come in lesser physical contact, they need to be reassured that they are as much a part of the team as others who are physically present in the office. Hence, including them through engagement activities can create a sense of CARE and belonging, giving them a positive outlook towards the organisation. Engaging employees through platforms such as features in internal newsletters, competitions, blog writing, neighbourhood volunteering programmes and virtual training brings in visibility of the employee and makes them feel included in the culture. Employees who feel included and recognised will always give their best. Have virtual suggestion platforms with effective response management. In fact, these are more secure than ethics and suggestion boxes as there are leaner chances of information being tampered with. A lot of trainers, buddies and mentors can be developed internally on a virtual platform who work from home but can, in turn, train people who work both in the office and from home. Celebrate small wins though desk claps and chats. Have a monthly social hour where people discuss everything except work. Connect with your teams on a personal and professional level and in turn, they will feel connected with you.

6. Improve mental health.

Social isolation can lead to mental health problems. No matter how advanced technology is, it can never replace watercooler conversations, coffee chats or sharing lunch boxes. An employee can also be continuously hallucinating about what is going on in the office, especially during the time of crisis. Working in isolation can lead to stress and depression. Although organisations emphasise on physical health programmes, very little attention is paid to mental health. Organisations encouraging remote working must take responsibility for the mental health of their employees. Inadequate mental health can have detrimental effects on our physical self, including blood pressure, racing pulse and heartbeat and hormonal imbalances, eventually causing loss of workdays, absenteeism or reduced productivity. Firstly, ensure that your employees are not overworked and get weekly offs. Secondly, ensure that they are counselled and trained on how to prioritise work, what is highly important and want can be carried forward to the next day. Thirdly, have an open-door policy and make yourself accessible to employees at all levels. This will make them feel that their problems are being addressed and will eliminate roadblocks, if any, in between the hierarchy. If a star employee has been underperforming, do not reprimand but try to understand why. Counsel, advice and help the employees stand back on their feet. Lastly, have remote wellness programmes and include them during the work hours schedule or half hour before work. Just like you have developmental trainers, also have councillors available 24/7 whom employees can approach. These should preferably be professionals outside the company.

7. Draw boundaries for working hours.

It is often assumed that since an individual is working from home, she/he is available 24/7. Although factually this data may be correct, one should have a line drawn between professional and personal time. Calling employees on week offs or after shifts should be avoided unless absolutely necessary. If you are a manager who likes working late hours or early mornings, do not assume that your subordinates should follow the same work routine as yours. Also, sending out emails late nights to subordinates can lead to huge anxiety in them. They may feel the urge to respond to your emails or begin to research data, just to satisfy their superiors and convince them that they are clued on. All this isn't necessary if you have confidence and trust in a relationship.

Draw shift hours for all employees who work from home and also communicate that they will need to work overtime or respond to urgent emails if need be, even after office hours. It would be best to code emails that are very urgent and important so that employees understand the seriousness of those emails and respond accordingly. Respect employees' cultures, religious holidays or prayer timings. However, give them a good balance between work and personal time as you have already had an agreement with them on remote working. Honour your commitment and draw the line.

8. Adopt new methods of reward and recognition.

With a growing percentage of remote workers, managers need new and innovative ways to establish a rapport with their Work From Home counterparts through incorporating rewards and recognition remotely. Send employees email appreciations marked to the rest of the team so that they feel their performance is being acknowledged and appreciated. Apart from email recognition, make sure that you personally tell them that they have done a good job over a virtual video or voice call. Send them gift vouchers that they can use either online or in their cities. Make certain that those gifts are something they value and not a choice of your own. Send flowers on their birthdays or even a bottle of wine.

Today everything is available at one's doorstep, hence, these little but meaningful gestures can create a high impact and make a world of a difference to an employee. Recommend employees for development programmes and help in their career growth. Don't just assume that because they work from home, they do not deserve to have development plans. Have simple yet motivating rewards, where not only employees but also their friends and families can see them being recognised. This can be done in magazines, on social media and other digital platforms.

Give star performers and good orators an opportunity to participate in webinars, seminars, media interviews and other talk shows. Share the stage with them when you receive awards and assure them that you couldn't have done it without them. Give them extra time off. This is something they would value and be grateful for. In today's modern day and age unlike our parents' generation, people don't work only for the money or job security. They pick up jobs that offer them both intellectual stimulation and emotional balance. Yes, money is important, but today's generation lives a lighter life and if you think it is only a big fat salary that can motivate them, then think again as you may have to change your ideologies about your culture.

9. Step up cyber security.

It is undoubtedly true that cyber security is the major deterrent for remote working. Longer online working hours increase cyber security risks. Business is being done over home ISPs, with unmanaged routers and printers, home automation systems and sometimes family, friends and children listening in on conversations or sharing computers, laptops or even phones while working for different organisations. Virtual private networks or VPNs, have become the new lifeline for many businesses. However, many home networks are already infected with malware or compromised hardware. A compromised identity or a machine can allow hackers to piggyback through the VPN.

It's critical to have strong authentication systems in place. Security does not mean eliminating all risks at a go. All threats may not be equally dangerous and may not be terminated at once. Risks faced today may be different from tomorrows, hence a strong information technology department should be developed that keeps its checks and balances at all times.

Remote managing of computer systems by information technology professionals with regular backups and update of anti-malware is of prime importance. Advisories, DOs and DONTs, standard operating procedures should not be just in black and white or communicated through email, but since this function involves technical jargons, frequent communication on these subjects needs to be disseminated. These should be in the form of animations, virtual training programmes or any other form that is impactful and showcases the directions to be followed meticulously. A twenty-four hour information technology helpdesk should be set up so that people can report any suspicious activities to the team no matter what part of the globe they are based at.

Another fear that organisations are weary about is employees stealing crucial data. However, I would advise organisations not to worry about this aspect too much as data can be stolen not only by remote employees but also by employees present at offices. Data can also be hacked at any juncture by hackers or competitors, hence data backup is more crucial than data security. Rather than worrying about loss of data and cutting off important search sites or pen drive hatches which, at times leave employees handicapped and frustrated, organisations should focus on policies that involve integrity or signing of disclaimers and take legal action against those employees who violate such agreements.

Although there may be many more methods of facilitating Work From Home, not everyone is cut out for this role. This could be because they are not able to inculcate seriousness in the role because of a million distractions or because they feel pressured as there are no boundaries between work and home. Let us understand some of the challenges employees face while working from home.

24

Challenges Employees Face While Working Remotely

1. Inadequate space

Although COVID-19 forced people to work from home, not everybody had the bandwidth of a private space within their homes. Most people worked out of their bedrooms or living rooms with disturbances such as traffic, children and pets coming along the way. Others may not have had luxe homes which made them scramble for a corner in the house to portray a fancy backdrop during a virtual meeting. This creates apprehensions, thus leaving the camera off for 80 percent of the meetings, in turn effecting face time communication and creating mental barriers about the employees focus.

Frequent disturbances can cause irritation and doubts in the mind of the employer, resulting into misunderstandings. Everyone may not have a three-bedroom house or a study to themselves. People could be living close to train or bus stations, marketplaces, places of worship and all these can create uninvited noise barriers. People may also have infants or young children in the house, pets like dogs or frequent visitors and all these reasons can increase the stress levels of employees as they feel they are not able to give their best while in front of the camera or over the phone as one never knows what disturbance could pop up.

There is a clear distinction between forced work from home because of circumstances and those who willingly opt to work from home. Hence, if you are an organisation considering a Work From Home or remote working policy, do ensure to run a check on whether the candidate has an adequate workspace, else this arrangement may never be fruitful.

2. Rising electricity, mobile and internet costs

If you have opted to work from home, be prepared to incur certain out-of-pocket expenses that would otherwise have been borne by the office. Phone and internet bills may rise way beyond reimbursement limits specified by the company. A spike in electricity bills is something you may have never anticipated, but be prepared. Do not bring these complaints to the management. In fact, be prepared to accept these and move on if you have chosen a remote working arrangement.

3. Working overtime

Flexibility comes with its pros and cons and one of the concerns you may have is not being able to switch off for the day. One has to accept that there is no visible boundary line between office and home and that one needs to be created. This again depends upon the agreement with the company you work for or the relationship you have with your boss. Working overtime can lead to mental fatigue, anxiety, frustration and even burnout. This, in turn, would again result in dealing with personal health issues, taking leave of absence undermining the preliminary reason of why you opted to work from home. Hence, good planning, prioritising and relationship management will help sort out this issue.

4. Over disciplining the family

Fear and anxiety while working from home may lead to developing strict rules and regulations for the family. This may result in arguments or misunderstandings that affect the mental health of the employee. Discipline while working from home is definitely crucial, but over discipline can be disastrous for the family. Don't let your workplace take over the house in a manner that your family feels that they are at your office day in and day out and not in the comfort of their homes. Don't make your children feel punished for nine or ten hours a day where they cannot make noise, sing, play music or take home tutorials. Disrupting family life to have the comfort of working from home just does not make sense. Choose to opt for remote working only if you can manage it effectively without impacting the well-being of your family.

5. Unhealthy snacking habits

Working from home gives you twenty-four-hour access to the fridge, kitchen and microwave. You have the power to eat whatever and whenever you desire. There is no doubt that we all live to eat, but the food we eat and the quantities we consume are pivotal to our health. Common ailments such as obesity, high blood pressure, diabetes, swollen joints, fatty livers are all a result of bad eating habits and mainly prevalent in people who have desk jobs. Hence, if your role encompasses sitting at your desk all day long, ensure that you do not succumb to unhealthy foods and eating patterns as you are putting your health at risk.

6. Fear of not being trusted

If you are an employee working from home, you may be frequently suppressed with the thought of what others may believe you do at home. There are some humans whose ignorance and mind set still leads them to believing that work cannot be performed from home. In case you end up with a boss like this, boy!........ you are in trouble. You will always be tracked and traced and then punished for every little thing that goes south. Just as an employer keeps certain factors in mind before making that Work From Home offer, candidates should also get a feeler of the individual they are reporting to. Ensure that your physical absence at the workplace does not affect your productivity and do not give reasons for your superiors to question your integrity. If you have opted for a work from home, stay at home. Don't let your boss catch you at a bar or at the marketplace during your shifts, whether in person or over the phone. Superiors, generally through experience, are pretty much aware of when people bluff. Just because they choose not to react doesn't mean they are unaware. Don't party hard thinking you have made a fool out of them. Do your bit with integrity and within time lines, go that extra mile to make things even more impactful and rest assured that 'credibility' will not be a challenging episode in your life.

7. Little or no appreciation

This again is one of the key challenges that people face when they work remotely. They are not part of the day-to-day culture, rewards and recognition, coffee room chats or celebrations which may lead to certain insecurities. These insecurities can cause mental stress, leading to make people believe that 'out of sight is out of mind'. Employees who work from home may be star performers but generally compromise on growth opportunities. This is something employees may have to live with until organisations widen their horizons and thus, job offers should be very thoughtfully accepted before deciding to opt for work from home.

However, if the nature of your job entails getting to the office whenever required or being out in the field for surveys and client meetings, there is no question about taking the back seat and swallowing those emotions where it comes to a promotion or a career development plan even if you work from home. If you have met with your KRAs, you have very well earned it, so go all out and ask for it because you deserve it.

Again, appreciation is a broad terminology and your superiors may be the type who really value you but do not write fancy letters thanking you for the things you do or send you flowers on your birthday. The very fact that they treat you with respect, encourage your thought process and thank you for your efforts are all clear indicators that you are being appreciated. So don't fight this aspect, understand, evaluate and discuss it.

Meghan was indeed blessed to have great bosses in her life. This she expresses with a big smile upon her face. You have to have visionary leaders as mentors and bosses who believe in your abilities. They are those leaders who don't bother about what you did today or any other day. They focus on results and witness your team perform. They know that team performance eventually leads to customer satisfaction, which leads to organisational growth. Most of us judge our bosses depending upon their mood swings as very often, waking up on the wrong side of the bed causes them to lash at everyone in the morning. What if you and your boss didn't have to see each other's face at a daily morning meeting? What if you get to see your boss once in a while, which makes both of you look forward to meeting each other and bonding together? Distance does make the heart grow fonder while out of sight is out of mind. How does one battle these situations and conclude on what's best?

25

Life's lessons revolve around flexibility and adaptability

There is always a calm after the storm. This gives us time to re-evaluate on how we could have done things differently or better. When the tsunami struck on 26th December 2004 in Thailand, most people were caught unaware and were preparing for Christmas. Many parts of the Asian continent, including parts of India, were engulfed with waves of such intensity that one had never heard of or dreamt of before. Every calamity or disaster has lessons to teach and these learnings only help us accept that life is unpredictable but can be made better if only we are prepared. On the other hand, one can never be prepared enough, but one can be brave and flexible enough to try new ways of living.

COVID-19 has changed our lives completely. Our children attend classes from home and have learnt more about computers and technology than classrooms ever taught them. Many of us who had apprehensions about home schooling have accepted that it is possible and may be even good for our children. Did you ever imagine not being able to hug your loved ones at a family get-together or a party, of treating others like untouchables or of having to put on a face shield or a mask every time you stepped out? What fun is life if we cannot be free? Today being free is being meticulous, extra cautious and fearful. However, if we only look at the fears and side line the positives, we wouldn't be playing it fair.

COVID-19 has brought many families together, taught us forgiveness, taught us to appreciate even one meal or value even a sip of water. It has showed us that we can live with the same wardrobe for months or even get a haircut at home. It has taught us new ways of doing things and different ways of making the same thing more interesting.

Life is not about what all we have, but it is about **who** we have and **what** we want. Success doesn't mean that you have to be put up high on a pedestal or appear on the cover page of *Forbes* magazine. To different people, it could be measured in different ways. Every human being has choices to make and the ones we make tend to be accepted as our destiny. But hey, it's never too late to turn around and change the way you live or operate. I would attribute being successful to being happy and there is nothing like being able to achieve it from the place you love the most . . . HOME.

So all you people out there who are working from home or even facilitating work from home, I am certain you will relate to everything I've said in this book. The idea of writing this book might have been triggered off by the pandemic, but the concept of remote working was not new to me. I had known Meghan for years now and she was able to do it over a decade ago in a country like India even during the era of emerging technology. If Meghan could do this perfectly well over all these years, it is definitely an eye-opener for all those still struggling with the decision of remote working. Today we have all the technology we desire to conduct meetings across the globe without having to travel. This technology has lately advanced to 3D and holographic inventions, which will simplify complex design handling jobs as well. Remote working is the future, but one should never miss out on that personal touch even if one is miles away. Your actions are governed by the choices you make. Flexibility comes with huge responsibility and the two must go hand in hand. Flexibility for survival and flexibility to achieve happiness are two separate sentiments that can be further debated. The bridge over the river Choluteca teaches us that we should not only learn to solve problems but be prepared for the problem to change itself. This simply means that flexibility and adaptability are the only factors that will not only help us survive but also make us happy human beings. The more rigid we are, the larger battles we fight and the more stress we endure. Times have changed, so has technology and work patterns. Why not make the best of what we have rather than sulk over what we do not? We may always bend backward and forward like a bamboo tree during strong winds, but what is most important is that we do not break. Flexibility has been showcased in many text book illustrations and famous quotes, but can be made a reality only when implemented. This can only occur if one has a strong foresight, an illuminating vision and is a strong believer of adaptability themselves.

I hope this read has given you insights to the ways the same things can be done differently. Work From Home is now the New Normal, is here to stay and one can confidently ***pave the highway to success from home***.

I would like to leave you with a famous quote by Charles Darwin that has great significance to the content of this book:

"It is not the most intellectual of the species that survives; it is not the strongest that survives; but the species that survives is the one that is able to adapt to and to adjust best to the changing environment in which it finds itself".